FUN-TASTIC CRAFTS for KIDS

Publications International, Ltd.

Four Books Means Hours of Fun!

Dear Parents,

Just about everyone has made a Thanksgiving turkey out of their handprint, homemade Valentines for their family and friends, or flowers out of tissue paper. But there are so many other crafty ways to fill your kids' days!

Fun-Tastic Crafts for Kids offers tons of fun, interesting projects that will keep your children busy throughout the year. From springtime flower bouquets and back-to-school projects to super summer flip-flops and way cool Christmas ornaments, kids can find crafts for all of their favorite holidays plus everyday projects to fill their days.

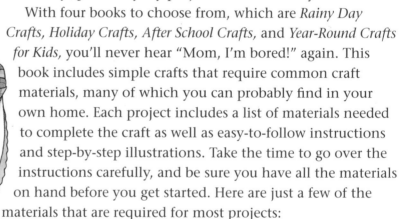

With four books to choose from, which are *Rainy Day Crafts, Holiday Crafts, After School Crafts,* and *Year-Round Crafts for Kids,* you'll never hear "Mom, I'm bored!" again. This book includes simple crafts that require common craft materials, many of which you can probably find in your own home. Each project includes a list of materials needed to complete the craft as well as easy-to-follow instructions and step-by-step illustrations. Take the time to go over the instructions carefully, and be sure you have all the materials on hand before you get started. Here are just a few of the materials that are required for most projects:

- Paper: Since many of the book's projects include patterns or stencils that will need to be traced and cut out, be sure to have plenty of tracing paper on hand. When a project calls for scrap paper, recycle some of that computer paper and junk mail you have lying around the house!

- Glue: Most projects call for craft, or white, glue. This is a waterbase glue that can be thinned for easy application. Fabric glue, which is not water-soluble, holds up better outdoors or in projects that will be washed. You'll also need a glue gun for some of the projects. Be sure to set the glue gun on low, and keep an eye on your child while he or she is using it.

- Paint: Waterbase acrylic paint is listed most frequently for the projects in this book. It is a vibrant form of paint that can be used on all surfaces. Acrylic paint dries permanently, but when wet it is easily cleaned up with water. Be sure your children clean painting tools thoroughly when they are finished painting.

- Chenille stems: Most chenille stems come in 12-inch lengths, so when a project calls for a chenille stem, that means a 12-inch stem.

- Art smock: Be sure your child wears a smock or one of your old shirts to protect clothes while working with paints and other messy materials such as clay.

Some children will be able to complete the crafts with little help, but there will be times when your assistance is needed. Other projects just need a watchful eye. So it's best if you and your child review each project together and then make a decision about your role.

Completing the projects in *Fun-Tastic Crafts for Kids* should be an enjoyable, creative, energizing experience for your child. Encourage kids to create their own versions of projects, using their imagination as a guide. And don't forget to admire and praise the wonderful results!

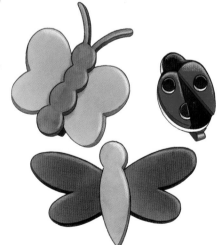

Hey, Kids!

There's no reason to ever be bored again. You can fill your time on rainy days, holidays, and after school. Use your creativity and your imagination, and, of course, the step-by-step guidelines, to make crafts you'll be proud to keep or give as gifts.

Fun-Tastic Crafts for Kids is filled with ideas for arts and crafts projects, many of which make great gifts for family and friends. Although we know you'll want to get started on the projects right away, please read these few basic steps before beginning.

- For any project or activity you decide to do, gather all your materials, remembering to ask permission first. If you need to purchase materials, take along this book, or make a shopping list so you know exactly what you need.
- Prepare your work area ahead of time, including covering any surface you work on with newspapers or an old, plastic tablecloth. Ask an adult if you're not sure whether to cover the kitchen table—but remember, it's better to be safe than sorry!
- Wear an apron or a smock when painting with acrylic paints; after the paint dries, it is permanent. If you do get paint on your clothes, immediately wash them with soap and warm water.
- Have an adult nearby to offer help if you need it. Adult help is *always* needed if you will be using a glue gun, a craft knife, an oven, or anything else that may be dangerous.
- Be careful not to put any materials near your mouth. And watch out for small items, such as beads, around little kids and pets.
- When using a glue gun, be sure to put it on the low-temperature setting. Do not touch the nozzle or the freshly applied glue; it may still be hot. And use the glue gun with adult permission only!
- Clean up afterward, and put away all materials and tools. Leaving a mess one time may mean you hear the word "no" the next time you ask to make something!
- Have fun, and be creative!

Pattern Perfect

Many of the projects featured in this book include patterns to help you complete the craft more easily. You may need to enlarge a pattern on a copier. The percentage is listed by the pattern. If there is no percentage listed, then the pattern is the correct size. There is no need to enlarge it.

When a project's instructions tell you to cut out a shape according to the pattern, trace the pattern from the book onto tracing paper, using a pencil. If the pattern has an arrow with the word *FOLD* next to a line, it is a half pattern. Fold a sheet of tracing paper in half, and open up the paper. Place the fold line of the tracing paper exactly on top of the fold line of the pattern, and trace the pattern with a pencil. Then refold and cut along the line, going through both layers. (Do not cut the fold.) Open the paper for the full pattern.

Ready, Set, Go!

All the projects presented in this book, from the simplest bookmark to the most elaborate beaded key chain, are just ideas to get you started crafting. Feel free to play around with the designs by changing the colors, choosing different materials, or embellishing in any number of unique ways. Once you are comfortable with these crafts, let your imagination really go wild and dream up some original crafts using these merely as a jumping-off point. There's no limit to what you can create!

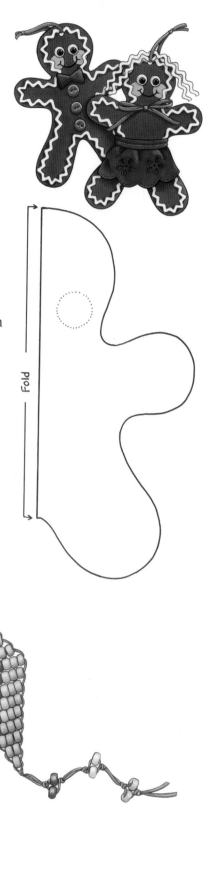

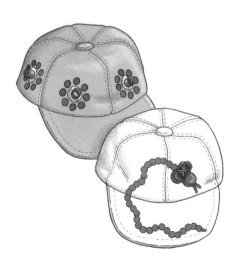

Contents

What You'll Need

Pink acrylic paint

Miniature water bottle, empty and dry

Pink craft foam

Scissors

Pink chenille stem

Low-temperature glue gun, glue sticks

4 pink poms, ¾ inch each

Black permanent marker

Perky Pink Piglet

Adult help needed

1 Pour a small amount of pink paint into the water bottle, and screw on the bottle cap. Roll the bottle around until the paint has completely coated the inside. Remove the cap, and pour the excess paint into the trash. Replace the cap.

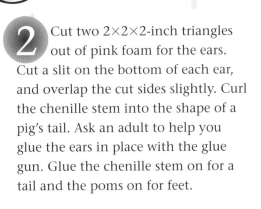

2 Cut two 2×2×2-inch triangles out of pink foam for the ears. Cut a slit on the bottom of each ear, and overlap the cut sides slightly. Curl the chenille stem into the shape of a pig's tail. Ask an adult to help you glue the ears in place with the glue gun. Glue the chenille stem on for a tail and the poms on for feet.

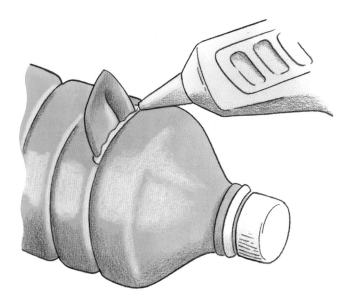

3 Draw the pig's eyes, eyebrows, and nostrils with the permanent marker.

4 Remove the bottle cap again, and let the paint inside dry overnight.

Stars and Stripes Pencil Wrap

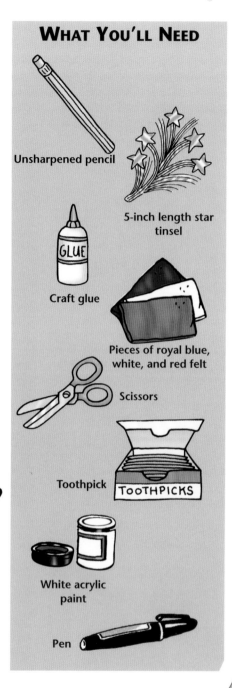

WHAT YOU'LL NEED

Unsharpened pencil

5-inch length star tinsel

Craft glue

Pieces of royal blue, white, and red felt

Scissors

Toothpick

White acrylic paint

Pen

1 Glue one end of the length of star tinsel to the metal part of the pencil eraser. Fold the tinsel over the top of the eraser, forming a loop, and glue down the other end of the tinsel to the other side of the metal part of the eraser.

4

2 Cut the royal blue felt into a 2¾×¾-inch strip. Using a toothpick, dot white acrylic paint onto the royal blue felt to make stars (about 3 rows, 10 dots in each row). Set aside to dry for 30 minutes.

3 Cut the white felt into a 1½×5-inch piece. Fold it in half lengthwise, bringing the shortest ends together. Use the pen to mark the halfway point on the inside of the fold. Unfold the felt, and lay it flat with the unmarked side facing up. Cut the red felt into 7 strips of ⅛×5 inches each. Glue a red felt strip along the top edge of the white felt piece. Glue on the other red strips, leaving a little bit of space between the strips so the white felt looks striped. Let dry for 30 minutes.

4 Turn over the white felt. Apply glue to the back side, then lay the pencil over the ink mark at the halfway point. Fold both sides of the felt around the pencil, covering up the end of the tinsel and any metal part near the eraser that is still showing. Align the ends of the white felt, and press firmly to hold.

Glue the royal blue felt piece in the upper left corner of the flag, wrapping the end around to the opposite side. Press firmly to secure. Sharpen the pencil when you are ready to write.

WHAT YOU'LL NEED

6 pieces adhesive craft foam: 1 black 5×4¾-inch sheet, 4 red 5×¼-inch strips, 1 green 4×4½-inch sheet

Plastic CD storage case

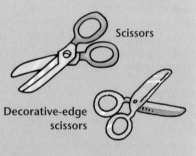

Scissors

Decorative-edge scissors

10 lengths 18-gauge plastic-coated wire: 5 red 3-inch lengths, 5 clear yellow 3½-inch lengths

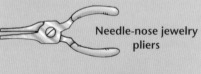

Needle-nose jewelry pliers

Permanent fine-point black marker

30 pre-cut hearts with adhesive backing: 10 red ¾×¾ inch, 20 white ⅝×⅝ inch

Tic-Tac-Toe to Go

1 Peel the paper backing from the black adhesive craft foam sheet, and press it onto the top of the CD case, matching corners at the side opening of the case. Cut ¼-inch red adhesive craft foam strips to lengths needed to form a square on the outside edges of the black craft foam, and attach it to the outer edges.

2 Cut the green adhesive craft foam sheet into ¼-inch strips using the decorative-edge scissors. One at a time, peel the backing and apply the green foam to the black craft foam to make a tic-tac-toe pattern as shown. Set the game board aside.

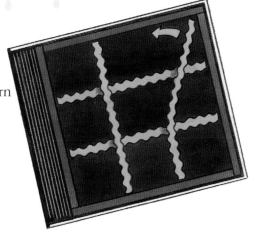

3 To make ladybugs, use needle-nose jewelry pliers to pinch and curl a loop at each end of all the red wires. Fold wires in half, turning the wire loops to create the body and antennae. With a black permanent marker, draw a line down the center of each red heart to make wings. Draw 3 black dots on each wing. Peel the paper backing, and attach 1 heart to the top of each wire body. Turn over and attach another heart on the back side of each bug, aligning the outer edges. Make 5 ladybugs.

4 To make butterflies, curl and bend the clear yellow wire to create the body and antennae. Because the yellow wire is longer than the red wire, the butterflies' antennae can be a little curlier than the ladybugs' antennae. Peel the hearts from the paper backing, and attach 2 white hearts to each wire for wings. Turn butterflies over. Press 2 more hearts onto the back sides of each butterfly, aligning the edges. Store the game pieces inside the tic-tac-toe case until you are ready to play. Make 5 butterflies.

Try This!
Use green hearts instead of red to make beetles instead of ladybugs. Butterfly wings can be different colors, too. Try coming up with new "bugs" for your game board using wire and adhesive craft foam shapes!

WHAT YOU'LL NEED

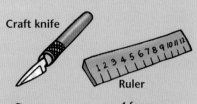
Craft knife

Ruler

Tracing paper

4 foam swimming noodles: assorted colors

Pencil

Adhesive craft foam sheets: assorted colors

Scissors

Fine-point permanent markers

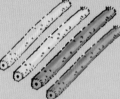
4 chenille stems, assorted colors, 12 inches each

½-inch yellow pom

Craft glue

Adhesive craft foam stars: assorted colors

Yellow ribbon

Fun-in-the-Tub Sailboats

Adult help needed

Pattern

1. Ask an adult to use the craft knife and ruler to cut a 1-inch slice from each color of the foam swimming noodles. This will create the donut-shape pieces needed for the boats.

2. Trace over the sail pattern shown on page 8, and cut it out. Place your pattern on adhesive craft foam sheets. Trace and cut out 4 sails from different colors. Don't peel the paper backing from the sails yet—you'll want to decorate them first.

3. Decorate your sails with markers or white adhesive craft foam. If you have white sails, as shown here, you might use a ruler to draw stripes on one and write your name on another. You can add numbers, squiggly lines, or dots just for fun. If your sails are a darker color, you can make stripes by cutting thin strips of another color of adhesive craft foam. Lay the sails flat, then peel the backing from the thin strips, and attach the strips to the sails. Cut strips to shorter lengths as needed.

4 One at a time, peel the paper backing from the sails. Center the bottom of the sail 1¼ inches from one end of a chenille stem. Fold the foam in half, wrapping it around the chenille stem. Align the edges, and then press the foam sides together. This will create the sail shape.

5 Fold the chenille stem ½ inch above the top of the sail, and twist once. Bend the rest of the chenille stem down along the side and bottom edge of the sail. Wrap the end of the stem around the chenille stem at the bottom of the sail to hold it in place. Insert the sail into a 1-inch foam noodle "boat." Repeat to make the remaining sailboats.

6 Add an accent to the top of each sailboat. You can glue a yellow pom to the chenille stem at the top of one sail, and tie a yellow ribbon at the top of another. Peel the backing from an adhesive craft foam star, and place it on the chenille stem at the top of another sail. Turn that sail over, and then peel the backing from another star of the same color. Press it onto the back side of the first star, aligning the edges. Peel the backing of a different star, and attach it on the side edge of a boat. To make a flag for the top of a sail, you can cut a ¼-inch strip of adhesive craft foam, peel the backing, and wrap it around the chenille stem at the top of the sail. Fold it in half, and align the edges before pressing together. Cut out a V shape at the end to make it look more like a pennant.

Try This!
Have races with your friends! Place your boats in a bathtub or swimming pool, and see which sails faster! Blow to create wind, and make your boat sail even quicker!

Stringing in the Rain

WHAT YOU'LL NEED

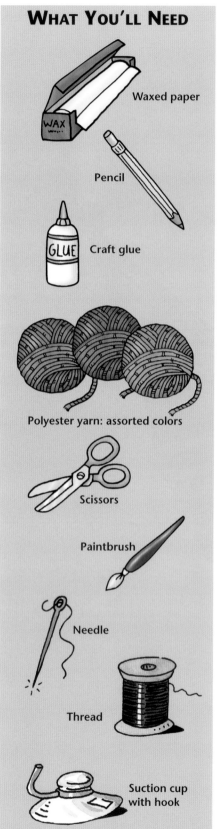

Waxed paper

Pencil

Craft glue

Polyester yarn: assorted colors

Scissors

Paintbrush

Needle

Thread

Suction cup with hook

1 Enlarge the butterfly pattern on page 13, and trace it onto waxed paper with a pencil. Divide the design into sections, and generously spread glue over 1 section. Starting in the middle of the section, gently lay yarn in a circular or side-by-side pattern until the section is entirely filled in.

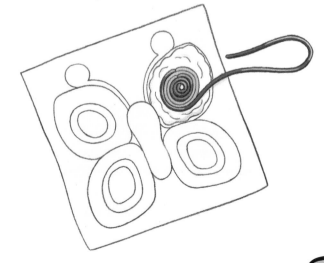

2 Cover the yarn in the finished section with a generous layer of glue. Spread it out evenly with the paintbrush until the area is completely covered.

3 Fill in the remaining sections the same way until the pattern is covered in yarn. Let the picture dry for 24 hours, and then trim the extra waxed paper from the outer edge of the design. At the top of the design, attach a hanging thread with a needle. Hang your design in any window with a suction cup.

Patterns

Try This!
Make other shapes on the waxed paper, such as the rainbow and balloons patterns provided below, and fill them in as well.

Enlarge patterns 165%.

Patriotic T-shirt

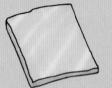

1. Launder the shirt before you begin so that the paint will adhere better; do not use fabric softener. Dry, then press the shirt with an iron if necessary. Place the shirt board inside the shirt, stretching the shirt over the shirt board. (This prevents paint from soaking through to the back of the shirt.)

2 Pour blue paint onto 1 plastic lid. Use a paintbrush to spread the paint into a circle about 4 inches across. Press the star sponge into the paint until the sponge surface is covered with paint but not saturated; then press the star sponge onto the white paper to practice stamping. Some white should show through the paint for a "sponged" look.

Dip the star sponge into the paint again before you make each stamp. When you're ready, randomly sponge about 10 stars on the shirt. Let the stars dry.

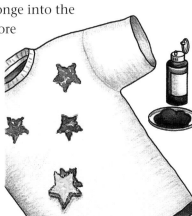

3 Attach a length of masking tape horizontally across the front of the shirt at the top. Overlap 3 or 4 more lengths of tape onto the first one until you have a 1¾-inch stripe of tape on the shirt. Put a light pencil mark on the shirt 1¾ inches down from the bottom of the tape. Repeat the taping procedure below that mark. Continue measuring and making 1¾-inch stripes of tape, and leaving 1¾-inch stripes of uncovered shirt between tape strips, until you get to the bottom of the shirt.

4 Prepare the red paint in the other plastic lid as you did with the blue paint. Practice painting with the rectangular sponge until you can do it neatly. Then begin stamping the uncovered bands of shirt between the bands of tape. Paint as close as you can to the blue stars, but be careful not to get any red paint on them. Continue stamping until all the bands on the shirt are painted red. Let the paint dry, and then remove the masking tape from the shirt. You can wear the shirt when it is dry, but do not wash it for 48 hours.

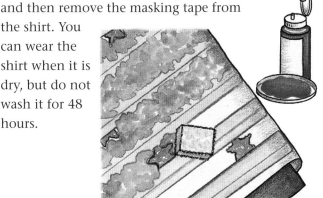

Pattern

Enlarge pattern 165%.

What You'll Need

72 inches of metallic craft cord, 2mm

Scissors

Split ring

Masking tape

½-inch green wood bead

4 blue wood beads, ¼ inch each

2 green wood beads, ⅜ inch each

2 green wood beads, ¼ inch each

Macrame Dragonfly Zipper Pull

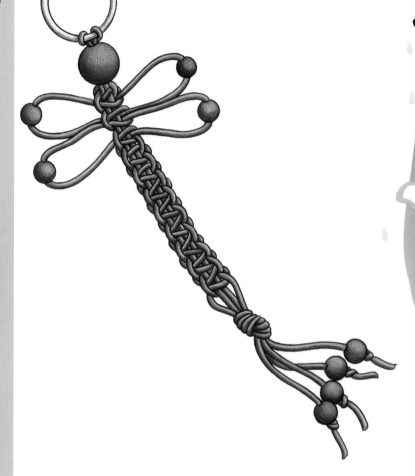

1 Cut a 24-inch length of metallic craft cord. Attach the cord to a split ring as shown, making both ends of the cord the same length. Tape the ring securely to your work surface. These will be your "holding cords."

16

2 Thread both strands through the ½-inch green bead, and move the bead up to the split ring for the dragonfly's head.

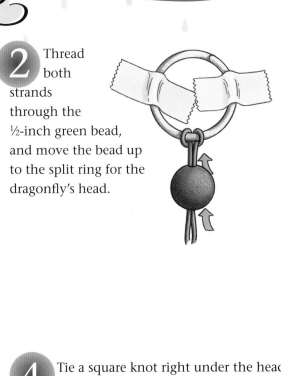

3 Cut a 48-inch length of craft cord. Slide it underneath the holding cords so each side is the same length. Position this just under the head bead. These will be your "working cords."

4 Tie a square knot right under the head bead. To tie a square knot, hold the working cords and holding cords together—the 2 holding cords should be in the middle and the 2 working cords should be on the outside. Number the working cords 1 and 4, and number the holding cords 2 and 3 as shown.

    a. Pass working cord 1 over holding cords 2 and 3 and under working cord 4. (The cords are shown as different colors, but all your cords will be the same color.)

    b. Pass working cord 4 under holding cords 2 and 3, then bring it up through the loop created by working cord 1. Tighten it.

    c. Pass working cord 1 over holding cords 2 and 3 and under working cord 4.

    d. Pass working cord 4 under holding cords 2 and 3, then bring it up through the loop created by working cord 1. Tighten it.

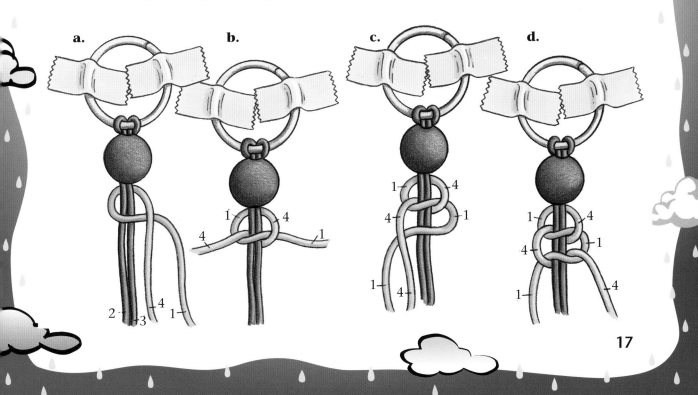

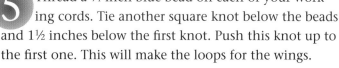

5 Thread a ¼-inch blue bead on each of your working cords. Tie another square knot below the beads and 1½ inches below the first knot. Push this knot up to the first one. This will make the loops for the wings.

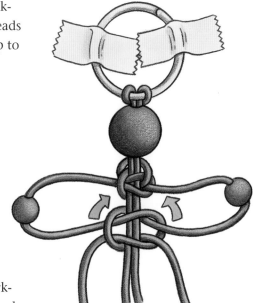

6 String a ⅜-inch green bead on each of your working cords. Tie another square knot below the beads and 1½ inches below the second knot. Push this knot up to the second one. This will make the second set of loops for the wings.

7 Tie 8 more square knots to make the body. With all the cords, tie a regular knot about 1 inch below the final square knot. On each cord, thread a ¼-inch bead. Tie a regular knot under each bead, and trim ends if necessary.

Undersea Wall Pocket

WHAT YOU'LL NEED

3 wood ovals,
1×2 inches each

3 wood hearts,
1×3 inches each

Small
paintbrush

Orange acrylic
paint

Double-sided tape

Aluminum
foil

Black
marker

Craft
glue

2 blue transparent
plastic plates,
9 inches each

Scissors

Hole punch

3½ yards
blue wire

Wire cutters

Ruler

Pencil

Craft foam: dark
green, light green

1 Paint one side of the wood ovals and hearts orange. Let dry, and then paint the other side. Let dry. Use double-sided tape to stick the wood shapes to a piece of foil to hold them still while you paint.

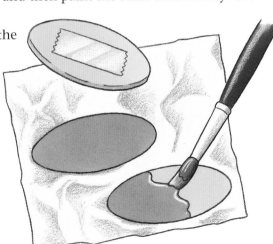

2 Outline the edges of the ovals and hearts with the black marker. Glue or tape the point of each heart to the end of the ovals to make fish tails. Draw a gill and eye on each fish.

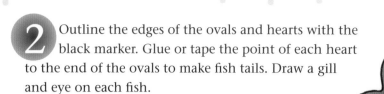

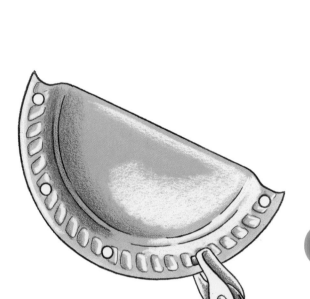

3 Cut 1 of the plates in half. Punch 5 holes spaced equally apart around 1 of the halves.

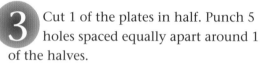

4 Place the half-plate on top of the whole plate so it forms a pocket. Use the black marker to mark the whole plate through the holes on the half plate. Separate the plates, and punch holes through the whole plate on those marks. Punch 2 more holes at the top of the whole plate for the hanger. Replace the half plate, lining up the holes to create a pocket.

5 Use wire cutters to cut five 18-inch lengths of wire. Thread a wire through each of the 5 holes at the bottom of the pocket, and twist wires below the plate to secure. Wrap each end of the wires around a pencil to form a coil. Coil the remaining wire, and attach each end to a top hole to form a hanger.

6 Cut thin wavy lengths of dark and light green craft foam. Glue or tape the strips to the plates to create seaweed.

7 Glue the wooden fish on the plates as desired.

Flower Garden

What You'll Need

Craft foam or cardstock: green, yellow, pink, orange

Scissors

Foam glue

Clothespins

Markers

4 craft sticks: green or regular

3 poms for flower centers

① Cut a strip of green craft foam or cardstock to 2×11 inches. Cut a jagged edge or fringe along one long edge for grass.

22

2 Glue the ends of the strip together. Hold the ends with a clothespin until the glue is dry.

3 Use markers to draw 4 flowers on the yellow, pink, and orange craft foam and 4 leaves on the green. Cut them out. If you are using plain craft sticks, color them green with a marker.

4 Glue 1 flower and 1 leaf to each stick, and glue a pom to the center of each flower except the tulip. When the glue dries, glue the flower stems behind the grass. Use clothespins to hold the stems to the grass until the glue sets.

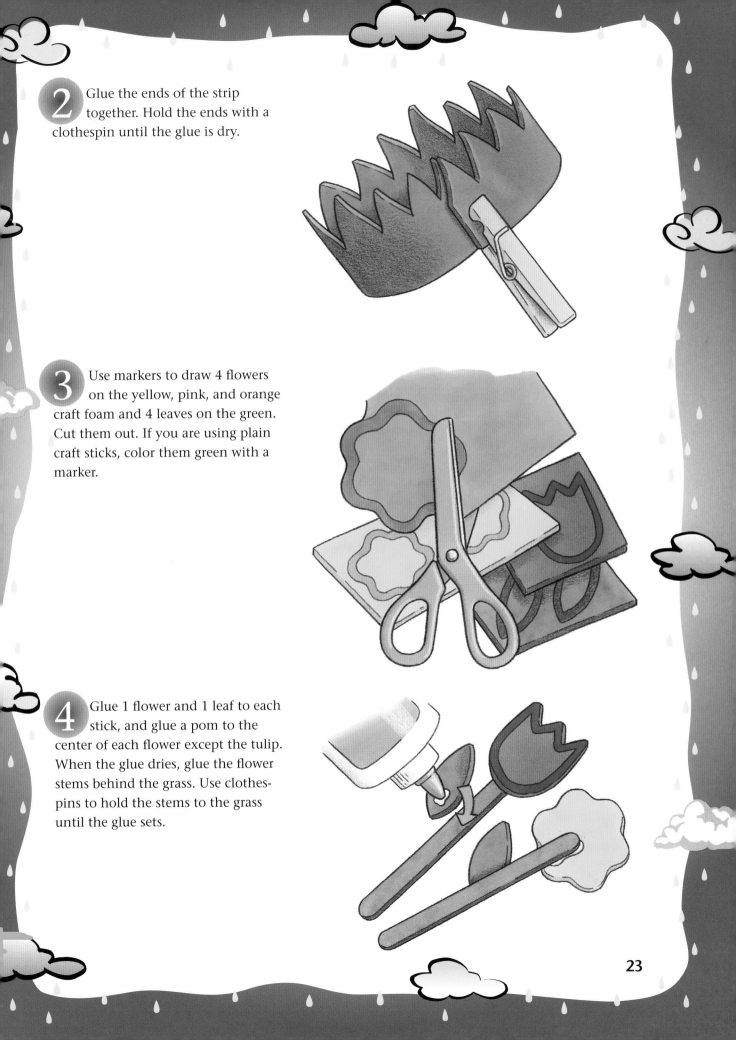

Checker Bulletin Board

Adult help needed

WHAT YOU'LL NEED

Bulletin board

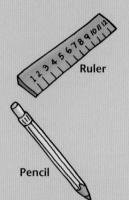

Ruler

Pencil

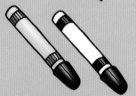

Red and black permanent markers

Checkers

Pushpins

Cement glue

1 Measure and mark lines 2 inches apart across and down the bulletin board to make squares for the checkerboard.

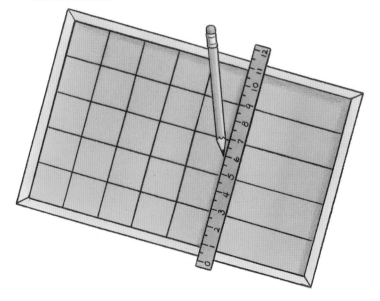

24

2 Color the squares with markers, alternating red and black.

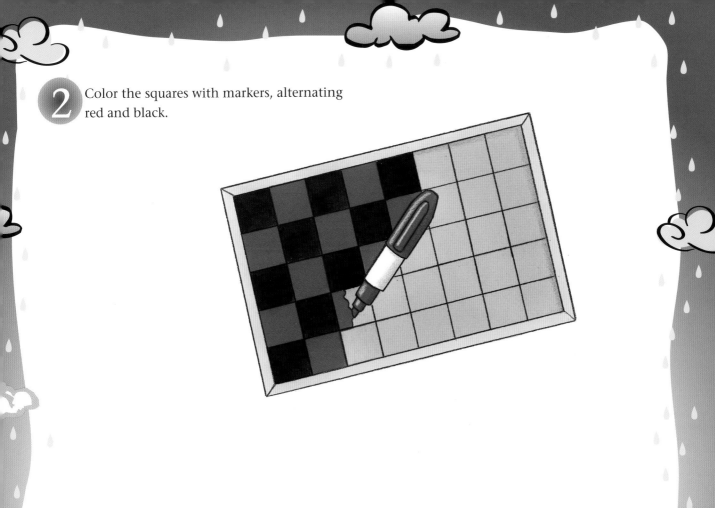

3 Ask an adult to help you glue the checkers to the pushpins with cement glue. Be sure you work in a well-ventilated area.

Puffy Paint Caps

What You'll Need

Fabric paints: velveteen-finish white, matte-finish purple (flower); velveteen-finish red, matte- and velveteen-finish green (snake)

Foam plates

Crayons: 1 jumbo, 1 regular

Plain baseball cap

Paper towels

Iron

4 inches neon pink plastic tubing, ⅜ inch diameter

Scissors

Craft glue

Pencil (snake only)

Toothpicks (snake only)

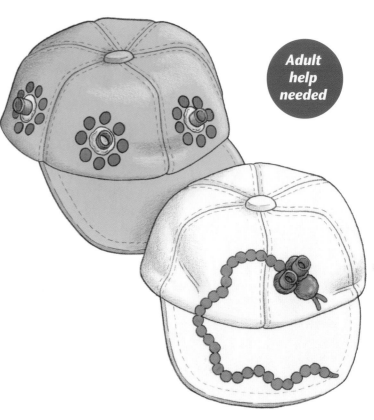

Adult help needed

Flower Cap

1 Pour a small amount of the white and purple fabric paint onto separate foam plates. Use the flat end of a jumbo crayon dipped in velveteen-finish white paint to make dots around the hat for the flowers' centers. Add more paint to the crayon as needed. Wipe off the crayon with a paper towel, and set it aside. Make petals by dipping the flat end of a regular crayon into the matte-finish purple paint. Dot 8 times around each flower center. Let dry 24 hours.

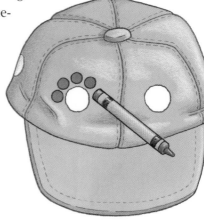

2 Ask an adult to help you use an iron to puff up the velveteen-finish paint. Set the iron on steam, and hold it 1 inch above the velveteen-finish paint until the paint puffs up. (Do not press the iron to the surface; just let the steam do the work.) Let it dry for 20 minutes. Cut small pieces of plastic tubing, and glue them onto the hat for the flowers' centers. Let the glue dry at least 4 hours before wearing.

Snake Cap

1 Pour red and both kinds of green paint onto separate plates. Draw a squiggly line on the hat with a pencil for where the snake's body will be. Dip the flat end of the regular crayon in the matte-finish green paint, and make dots along the pencil line until you reach the head area. Wipe off the crayon with a paper towel. Use the flat end of the jumbo crayon dipped in velveteen-finish green paint to make 3 slightly overlapping dots for the head. Wipe off the crayon. Dip the side edge of a toothpick into red paint, and apply paint onto the hat near the snake's mouth for the tongue. Use a toothpick dipped in velveteen-finish green to make a tail. Let dry 24 hours.

2 Repeat step 2 of the Flower Cap to puff velvet-finish paint. Cut 2 pieces of tubing, and glue them on the head for eyes.

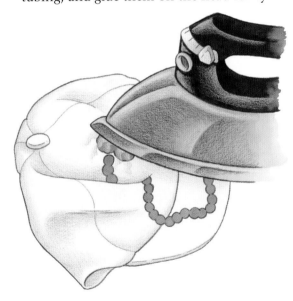

27

Wood frame

Adult help needed

3 yards lightweight ribbon, ½ inch wide

Low-temperature glue gun, glue sticks

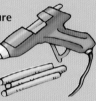

Scissors

Silk daisies: pink, white

Photo

Heavy-duty clear packing tape (optional)

Daisy Frame

1 Take apart the wood frame, and set aside the frame backing and the glass. Glue one end of the ribbon to the top middle of the back side of the frame. Wrap the ribbon around the frame, overlapping the ribbon edges to hide the wood. Pull the ribbon taut, but make sure there is enough give so that the frame backing will still fit in the frame.

2 When the frame is completely covered, cut the ribbon, and glue the end to the back of the frame.

3 Lay the frame right side up on a flat surface. Position the daisies as desired on the front of the frame. Once you're happy with the design, glue the flowers in place.

4 Press the glass back into place, position the photo inside, and fit the frame backing into place. If the backing no longer fits, use heavy-duty clear packing tape to secure the backing to the frame.

Lizard Bookmark

WHAT YOU'LL NEED

Thick, stiffened green felt, 9×12 inches

Fine-point marker

Craft glue

Scissors

Red felt, 1½×½ inches

Magnet strip

Acrylic paint: green, light green

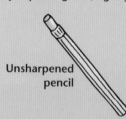

Unsharpened pencil

Small wiggle eyes

1 Use the marker to trace the lizard pattern on page 31 twice onto the thick, stiffened felt. Cut out the 2 lizard shapes.

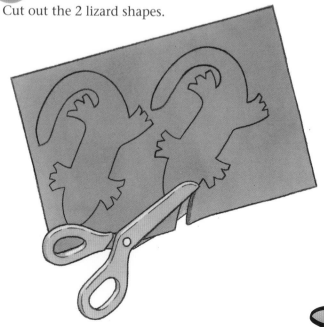

2 Place the lizard shapes on top of one another, and line them up. Glue the 2 lizard shapes together around the edges below the front legs. Leave front legs and head unglued.

Patterns

31

3 Trace the tongue pattern on page 31 on the red felt, and cut it out. Glue the tongue to the inside top of the mouth so it sticks out a little. Cut 2 small strips of magnet, and glue 1 strip to each side of the inside of the lizard's head.

4 Dip the eraser end of the unsharpened pencil into the green paint, and stamp a spot onto the lizard. Repeat stamping until you have as many spots as you would like. Repeat with the light green paint. Let the paint dry.

5 Glue the wiggle eyes onto the lizard's head. Use the magnetic head to hold your place in your book.

WHAT YOU'LL NEED

Plastic visor: green (frog), yellow (sunflower)

Pencil

Scissors

Craft foam: green, white, black, red (frog); yellow (sunflower)

GLUE

Glue

Fabric Paint

Fabric paint: black, green (frog); red, yellow (sunflower)

Super Summer Visors

Frog Visor

1 Trace and cut 2 large frog eye shapes out of green craft foam, using the pattern on page 34. Put a little glue along the straight edge of each cutout, and glue the foam to the top edge of the green visor. Let dry.

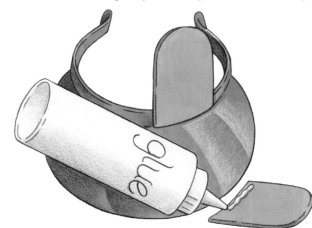

2 Use the patterns below to cut 2 large circles out of white craft foam and 2 smaller circles out of black craft foam. Glue each white circle to each green frog eye shape. Glue the black circles onto the white circles.

3 Draw 2 nostrils on the visor with the black fabric paint. Outline the green of each eye with green fabric paint. Use the pattern on this page (the same pattern used previously for the eyes) to trace a tongue shape on the red craft foam, and cut it out. Glue the tongue along the curved edge of the visor.

Patterns

Sunflower Visor

1 Using the pattern below, trace and cut out 9 petal shapes from the yellow craft foam. Glue them along the underside of the curved edge of the yellow visor.

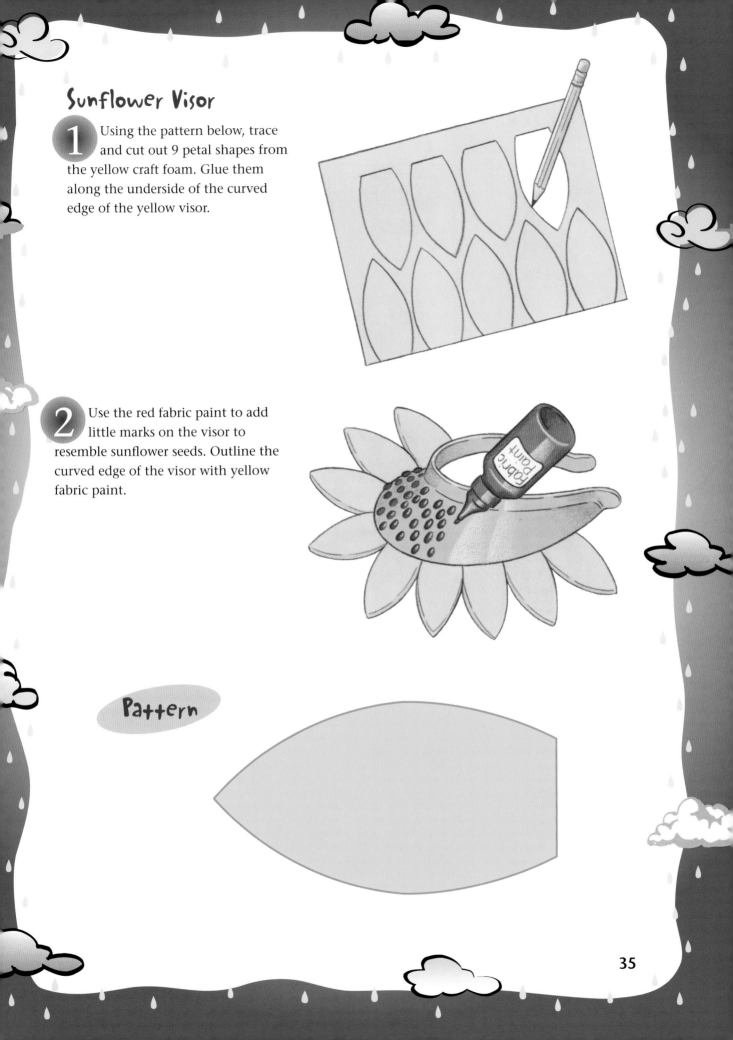

2 Use the red fabric paint to add little marks on the visor to resemble sunflower seeds. Outline the curved edge of the visor with yellow fabric paint.

Pattern

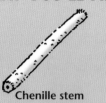

Chenille stem

Low-temperature
glue gun, glue sticks

Clean foam tray

Scissors

Paint

Paintbrush

Note card

Clear glitter

Sparkly Stamped Note Cards

Adult help needed

1 Bend the chenille stem to create a fun design you
like, such as a heart. Use the glue gun to add glue
to one side of the bent chenille-stem design, and then
attach it to the foam tray. Hold it there for 10 seconds.
This will create a stamp.

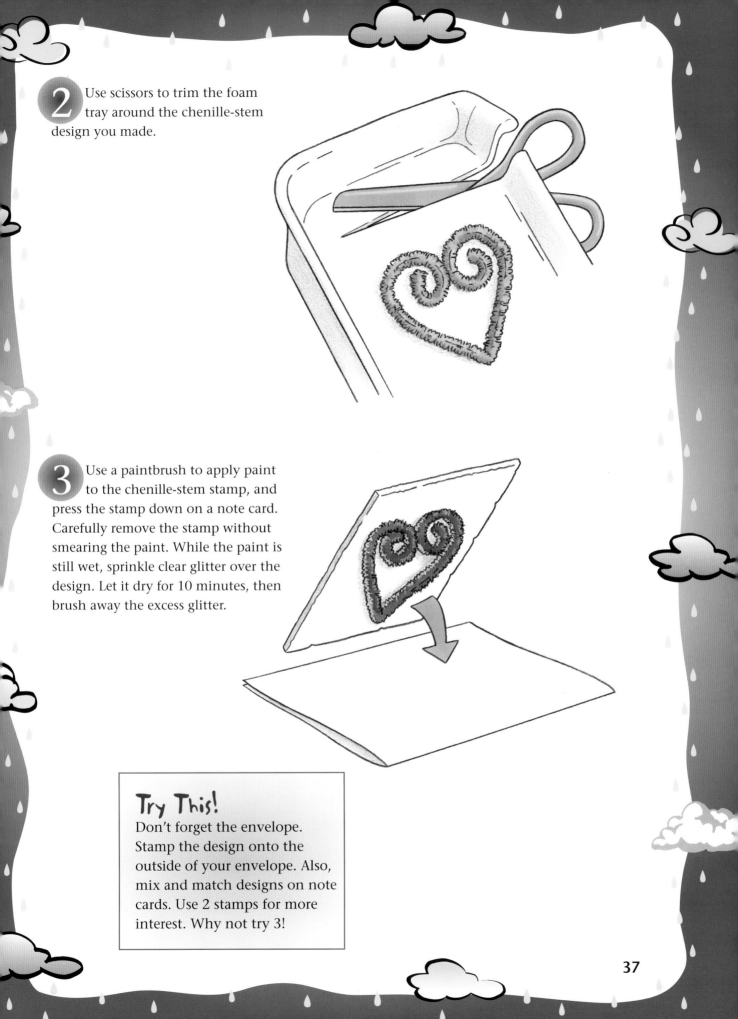

2 Use scissors to trim the foam tray around the chenille-stem design you made.

3 Use a paintbrush to apply paint to the chenille-stem stamp, and press the stamp down on a note card. Carefully remove the stamp without smearing the paint. While the paint is still wet, sprinkle clear glitter over the design. Let it dry for 10 minutes, then brush away the excess glitter.

Try This!

Don't forget the envelope. Stamp the design onto the outside of your envelope. Also, mix and match designs on note cards. Use 2 stamps for more interest. Why not try 3!

WHAT YOU'LL NEED

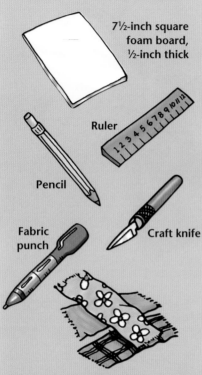

7½-inch square foam board, ½-inch thick

Ruler

Pencil

Craft knife

Fabric punch

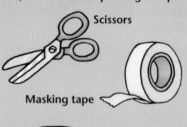

Fabric: two 2¾-inch squares and two 3-inch squares blue print; two 2¾-inch squares and two 3-inch squares pink print; four 3×5-inch pieces green print

Scissors

Masking tape

4-inch length satin ribbon, ⅛ inch wide

Low-temperature glue gun, glue sticks

7¼-inch square white poster board

9 buttons, ½ inch diameter

Beautiful Button Quilt

Adult help needed

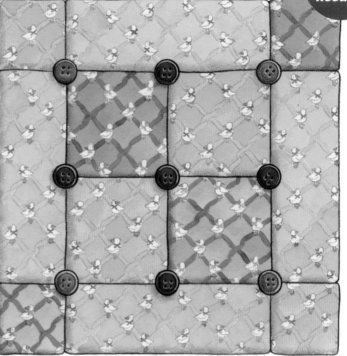

1 Measure and mark the lines on the foam board with the pencil as shown below. Ask an adult to score the lines about ⅛ inch deep with the craft knife. Then run the flat end of the fabric punch along the scored lines to make them slightly larger.

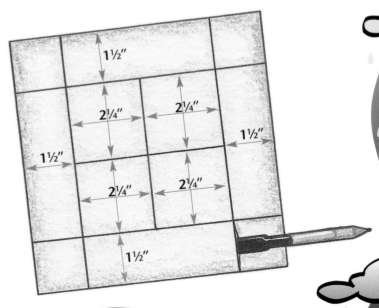

1½" 2¼" 2¼" 1½" 1½" 2¼" 2¼" 1½"

2 Set a 2¾-inch square of fabric on the foam board, centered over one of the inner squares made by the scored lines. Using the flat side of the fabric punch, carefully poke the fabric into the middle of each of the 4 scored lines of the square to hold the fabric in place. Continue pushing the fabric into the scored lines all the way around the square. Use scissors to snip off any fabric edges that are too long to tuck in. Put the remaining fabric pieces into the foam board in the same way (see the illustration for placement). The outside edges of the 8 pieces of fabric on the sides of the foam board will be loose.

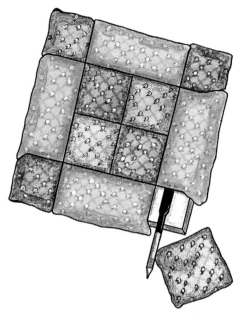

3 Working with the corner pieces first, carefully fold the loose edges of fabric around the back of the foam board, and tape them securely. Fold the ribbon in half to form a loop, and glue the 2 ends to the back of the foam board for a hanger. Glue the poster board onto the back of the foam board so the fabric edges are covered.

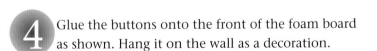

4 Glue the buttons onto the front of the foam board as shown. Hang it on the wall as a decoration.

Snazzy Sneaker Set

WHAT YOU'LL NEED

White sneakers

26 red puffy stars, ¾ inch each

27 blue puffy stars, ¾ inch each

Low-temperature glue gun, glue sticks

White painter's cap

Glittering silver dimensional paint

2 (size H) wood circles, ¾ inch each

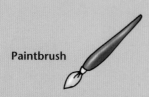
Paintbrush

White acrylic paint

2 sets earring posts and backs

Adult help needed

1 Plan how to arrange 5 red and 6 blue stars on 1 shoe as shown. Apply glue to the back of each star, and place on a shoe. Align and glue together 2 red puffy stars back to back just above the end of 1 shoelace, sandwiching the shoelace between the stars. Repeat with 2 blue puffy stars for the other end of the shoelace. Repeat for the second shoe. Similarly position and glue 10 blue and 11 red stars on the painter's cap.

2 Squeeze-paint 3 glittering silver rays shooting out from each star on the shoes and the painter's cap. Let the paint dry.

3 For the earrings, paint wood circles with 2 coats of white paint. Let the paint dry between coats. Apply glue to the back of a blue puffy star and place on a wood circle. Apply glue to center back of the wood, and place the earring post into the glue. Repeat to make a second earring with the puffy red star.

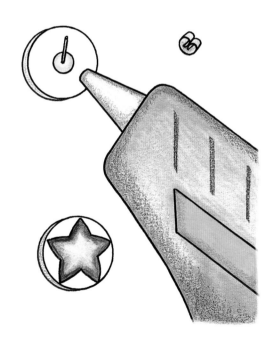

WHAT YOU'LL NEED

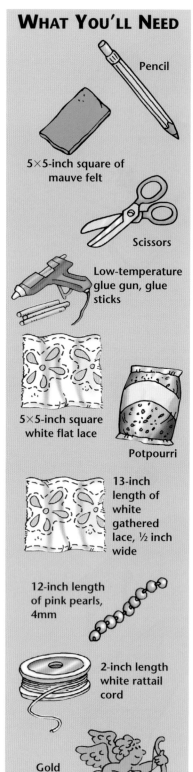

Pencil

5×5-inch square of mauve felt

Scissors

Low-temperature glue gun, glue sticks

5×5-inch square white flat lace

Potpourri

13-inch length of white gathered lace, ½ inch wide

12-inch length of pink pearls, 4mm

2-inch length white rattail cord

Gold charm

Adult help needed

1 Using the pattern on page 43, trace and cut 1 felt heart and 1 flat lace heart. Glue the 2 hearts together along the edges, leaving 2 inches along the side unglued. Gently stuff the heart with potpourri, and then glue the opening closed.

2 Glue the gathered lace along the outer edge of the felt side of the heart, starting at the top center. Glue the string of pearls to the outer edge of the lace side of the heart, starting at the top center—be sure to cover the glue line that attaches the flat lace to the felt.

3 To make a hanger, fold the rattail cord in half to form a loop, and glue the ends to the felt side of the heart.

4 Glue the gold charm in the middle of the lace side of the heart.

Pattern

fold

Foam Frogs

What You'll Need

Craft foam:
green, light green

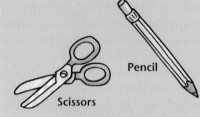

Scissors

Pencil

Acrylic paint: light yellow, white,
pink, red, black

Paintbrush

8 wood circles:
4 medium, 4 small

Craft glue

Black marker

2 suction cups

1 Enlarge and trace the frog pattern on page 45 onto both the green and light green craft foam, and cut them out.

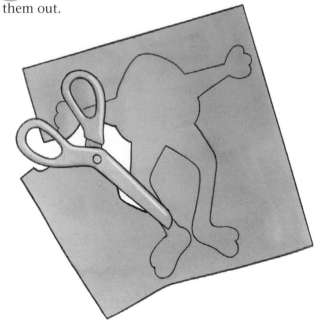

44

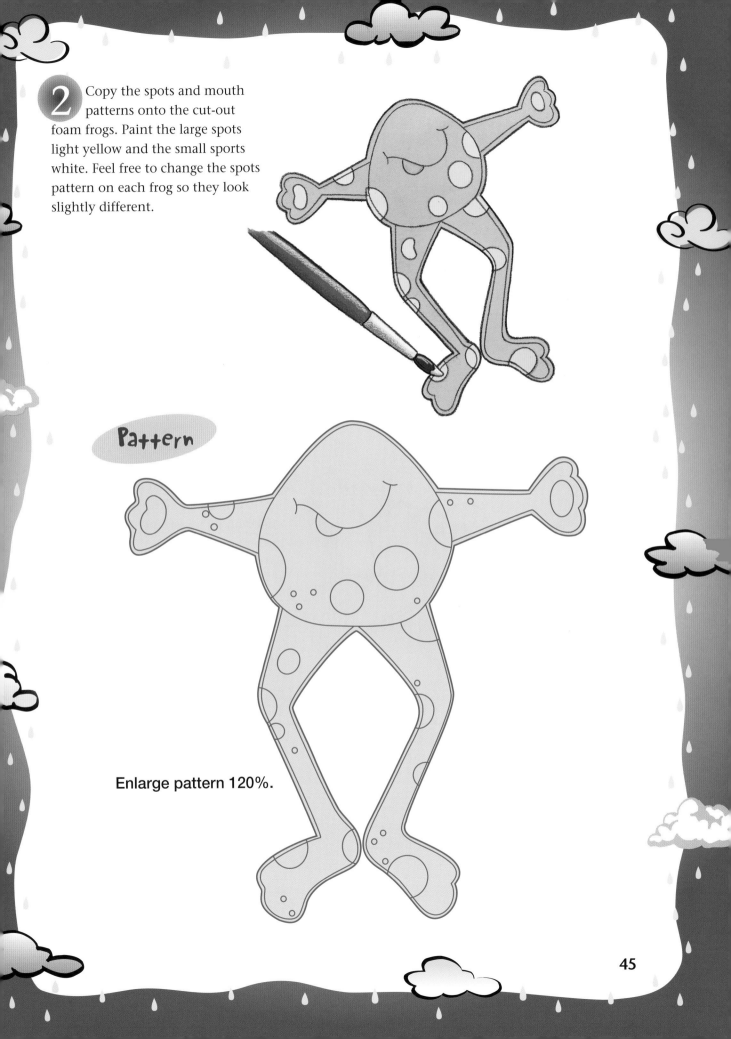

2 Copy the spots and mouth patterns onto the cut-out foam frogs. Paint the large spots light yellow and the small sports white. Feel free to change the spots pattern on each frog so they look slightly different.

Pattern

Enlarge pattern 120%.

3 With the black marker, outline the mouths and draw lines on the yellow spots. With a dry brush, lightly paint the cheeks pink. Paint the tongues red. Add black lines to 1 frog's tongue.

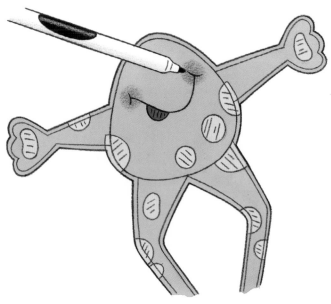

4 Paint the medium wood circles white and the small wood circles black. Let dry. Glue the small black circles on top of the medium white circles for the eyes. Outline the eyes with the black marker. Glue 2 eyes to the top of each frog's head.

5 Glue the suction cups to the back of each frog. Attach the frogs to a window or a mirror.

What You'll Need

2 round ball knobs: 1½ inch, 2 inch

Drill and ³⁄₁₆-inch drill bit

Acrylic paint: gray, black, white, red

Paintbrushes

Low-temperature glue gun, glue sticks

2 small wood knobs: ¾ inch, 1 inch

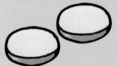
4 wood circles: ¾ inch each

Black marker

11 inches black coated wire, 18 gauge

Wire cutters

Two Quiet Mice

Adult help needed

1 Place the round ball knobs on the flat sides. Have an adult drill a hole in each for inserting the wire tails.

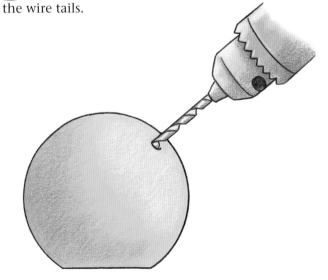

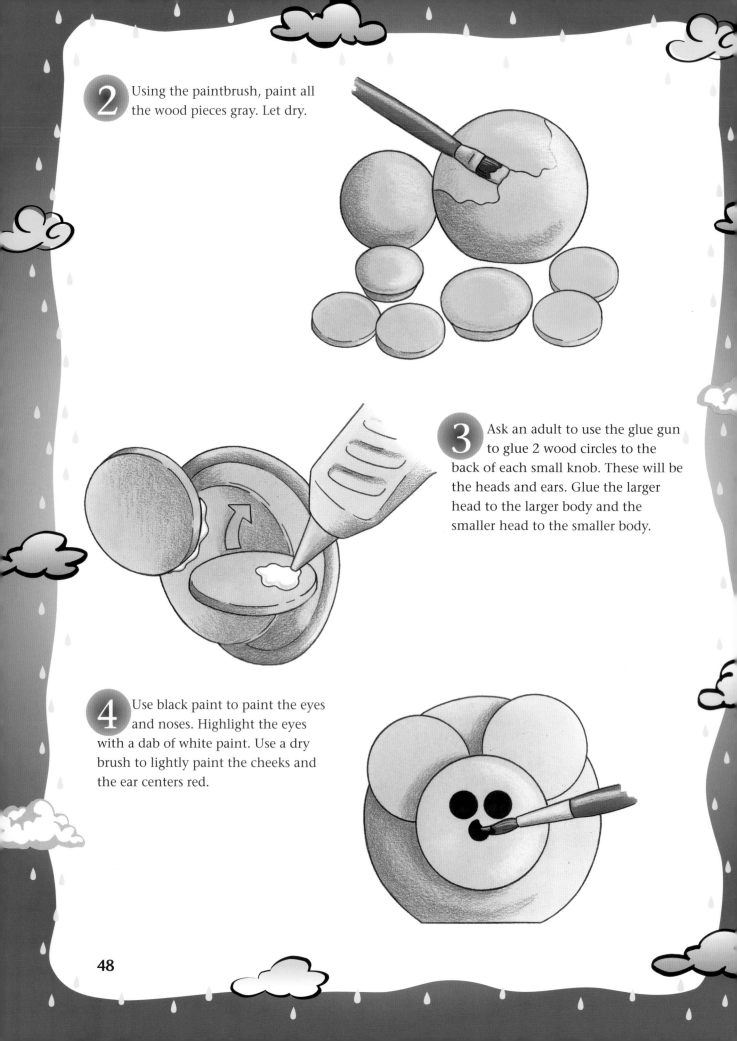

2 Using the paintbrush, paint all the wood pieces gray. Let dry.

3 Ask an adult to use the glue gun to glue 2 wood circles to the back of each small knob. These will be the heads and ears. Glue the larger head to the larger body and the smaller head to the smaller body.

4 Use black paint to paint the eyes and noses. Highlight the eyes with a dab of white paint. Use a dry brush to lightly paint the cheeks and the ear centers red.

5 Outline the ears and faces with the black marker. Draw on whiskers and eyebrows.

6 Cut a 6-inch length of wire for the larger mouse's tail and a 5-inch length for the smaller mouse's tail. Twist 1 end of each tail around the marker to make a swirl. Poke the uncurled end of the wires inside the holes drilled earlier, and glue them inside. Slide photos or notes into the wire swirls.

Safety Pin Bracelet

25 to 35 gold safety
pins, 1 inch each

200 to 250 faceted
beads, 4mm each

Needle-nose pliers

Memory bracelet
wire

100 to 125 round gold
beads, 3mm each

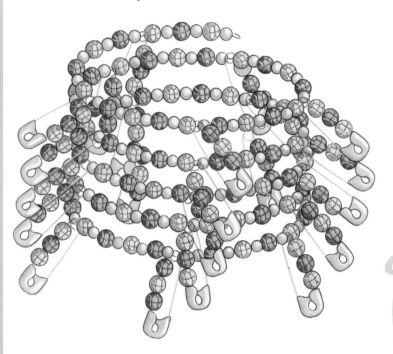

1 Open up the safety pins, and slide 3 faceted beads on each in random combinations. Close the safety pins, and pinch the heads with the needle-nose pliers. This will flatten the heads to keep the safety pins from opening up.

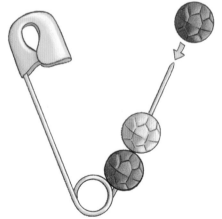

2 With the needle-nose pliers, bend 1 end of the memory wire into a small loop to keep beads from sliding off the end.

3 Alternate stringing on faceted beads and gold beads. After every 6 or 7 beads, string on a beaded safety pin. Continue adding pins and beads in this manner until you have filled the memory wire. Bend the other end of the wire into a small loop with needle-nose pliers.

What You'll Need

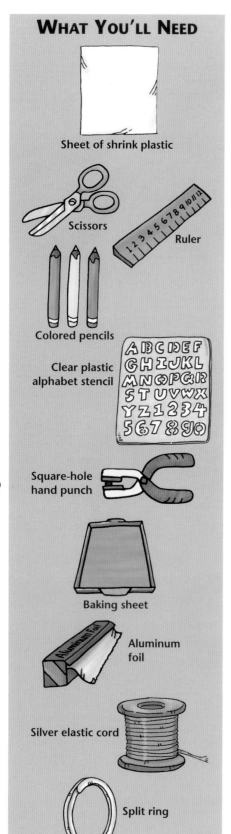

Sheet of shrink plastic

Scissors

Ruler

Colored pencils

Clear plastic alphabet stencil

Square-hole hand punch

Baking sheet

Aluminum foil

Silver elastic cord

Split ring

Neat-O-Shrinky Jewelry

Adult help needed

Bracelet

1 To make a bracelet, cut the shrink plastic into 7 squares, 2×2 inches each. Round the corners of the squares so they aren't sharp. Use 2 colored pencils to draw a border on the dull, rough side of each square. Color the borders of 3 squares with 1 color and the borders of the other 4 with a second color.

2 Choose a letter for 3 of the squares, maybe your initials. Lay the alphabet stencil sheet over each of the squares, and make sure the letter is centered. Color in that letter with a third color.

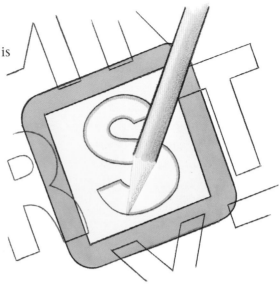

3 Draw and color a flower in the center of the remaining 4 squares. Color the remaining space in each square.

4 Punch a hole with the square-hole hand punch in the 4 corners of each square piece.

5 Bake according to the directions on page 56.

Zipper Pull

1 To make a zipper pull with your name on it, use the alphabet stencil to trace the letters of your name in 1 color on the dull, rough side of the shrink plastic. Arrange the design of the letters so they touch and are stacked on top of each other. Choose another color to fill in the letters.

2 Cut your name out of the plastic. Make a slit in the film between some of the stacked letters, but be sure not to cut them apart. When the design shrinks, the letters will pull away from each other, giving the name a stretched, hanging look.

3 With the square-hole hand punch, punch a hole in the top of the zipper pull.

4 Bake according to the directions on page 56.

Key Chain

1 To make a skateboard key chain, lay the shrink plastic over the pattern below, and trace it on the film's dull, rough side.

2 Use colored pencils to color in the skateboard's design and wheels.

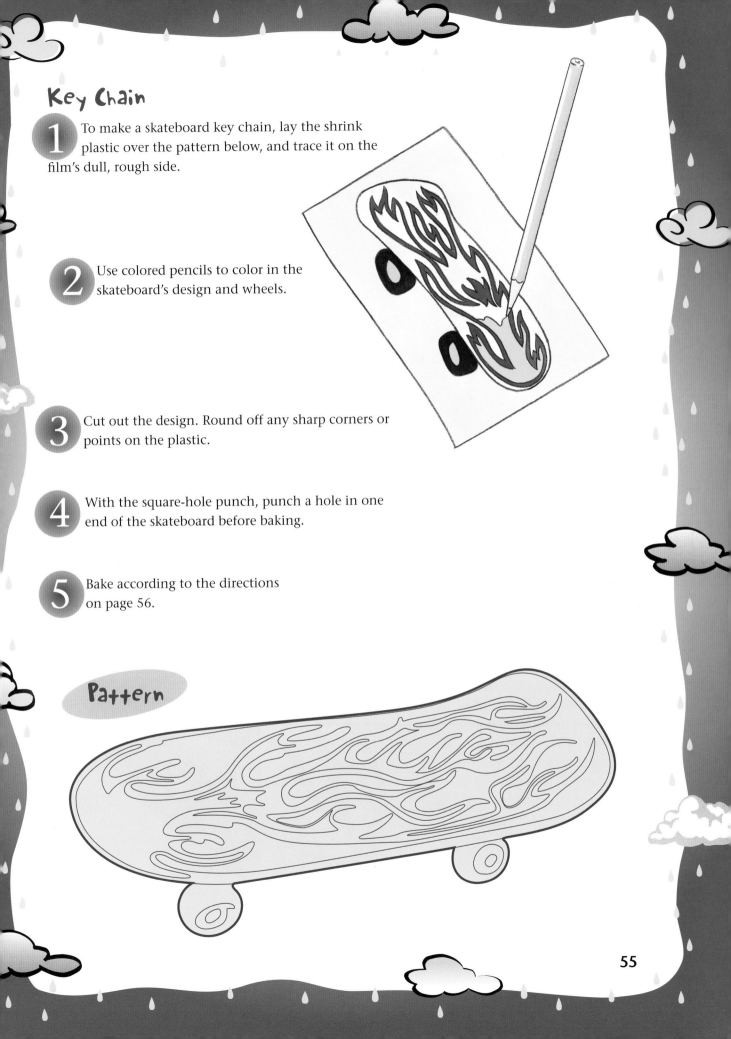

3 Cut out the design. Round off any sharp corners or points on the plastic.

4 With the square-hole punch, punch a hole in one end of the skateboard before baking.

5 Bake according to the directions on page 56.

Pattern

Baking

1 Read and follow the instructions that come with the shrink plastic, particularly the tips and cautions for baking.

2 Cover a baking sheet with aluminum foil. Place each of the pieces on the baking sheet, and have an adult bake them in a preheated oven. Watch the pieces through the oven window—they will curl up and lay flat again. This will happen quickly, so don't walk away.

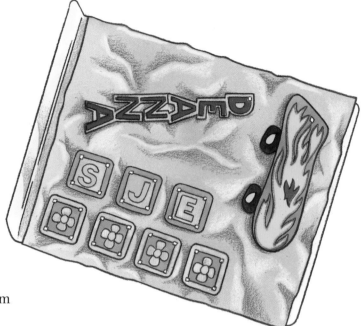

3 When the pieces are finished, have an adult remove them from the oven, and allow them to cool.

4 Attach a length of silver elastic cord or a split ring to the zipper pull and skateboard.

5 To put the bracelet together, cut 2 pieces of silver elastic cord to 8 inches. Thread 1 cord through the top holes on the square pieces and the other cord through the bottom holes. Make sure the cord runs along the back of the pieces. Alternate the flower design with the initials. Fit the bracelet to your wrist, and tie a knot with the 4 end pieces of cord. Trim any extra cord.

56

Contents

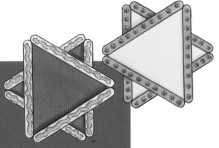

Valentine Candy Magnet

Adult help needed

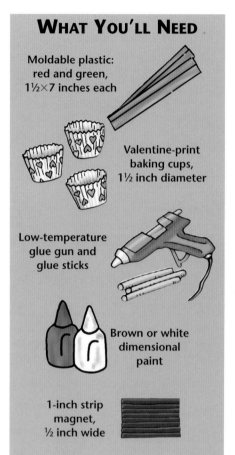

WHAT YOU'LL NEED

Moldable plastic: red and green, 1½×7 inches each

Valentine-print baking cups, 1½ inch diameter

Low-temperature glue gun and glue sticks

Brown or white dimensional paint

1-inch strip magnet, ½ inch wide

1 Place the strips of moldable plastic in warm water until they are soft. Knead and mix the 2 strips together until they are a uniform brown color. You may have to resoften the plastic a few times to remove all the streaks of red and green. Roll the plastic between your palms to form a smooth ball. Flatten one side of the ball slightly by gently pushing it onto your work surface. Allow the plastic ball to set.

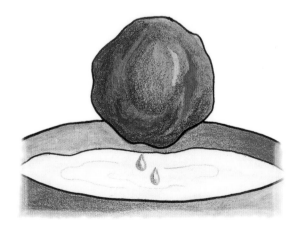

2

2 Glue the flattened side of the ball to the bottom of the baking cup. Glue the sides of the baking cup to the sides of the ball in 3 or 4 places. Paint wavy lines across the top of the ball with the dimensional paint. Let dry.

3 Glue the magnet strip to the bottom of the baking cup. Repeat all the steps to fill your refrigerator with delicious-looking "candy" magnets!

Did You Know?

The original St. Valentine lived during the time of Roman Emperor Claudius II, who wanted the men in the army to stay unmarried. But St. Valentine would secretly marry the men and their sweethearts.

WHAT YOU'LL NEED

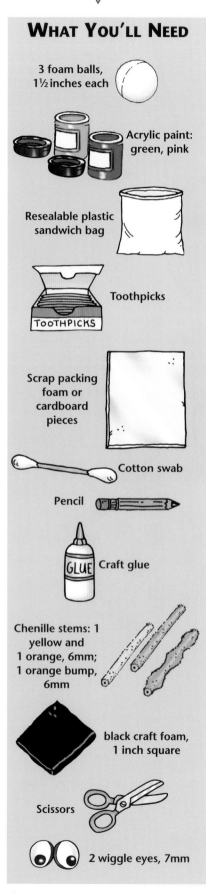

3 foam balls, 1½ inches each

Acrylic paint: green, pink

Resealable plastic sandwich bag

Toothpicks

TOOTHPICKS

Scrap packing foam or cardboard pieces

Cotton swab

Pencil

GLUE Craft glue

Chenille stems: 1 yellow and 1 orange, 6mm; 1 orange bump, 6mm

black craft foam, 1 inch square

Scissors

2 wiggle eyes, 7mm

1 To make the hat brim, flatten a 1½-inch foam ball by pushing it down onto your work surface. Make it even thinner by picking it up and squeezing it between your fingers. To make the top of the hat, gently flatten the top and bottom of another 1½-inch foam ball. Roll side edges on the table, pressing and then squeezing, to form the top portion of the hat. Place the top of the hat on the brim and twist to sand lightly. This will help the pieces lie flush when the hat is finished.

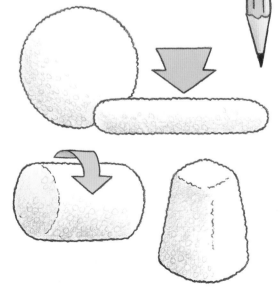

2 Pour a small amount of green paint into the resealable plastic bag. Place the hat pieces in the bag, and seal the bag. Shake the hat pieces around inside the bag until they are completely coated with paint. Remove the pieces from the bag with toothpicks. (Be careful to remove the hat bottom-end up to avoid leaving a toothpick hole in the top of the hat.) Insert the opposite end of the toothpick into a piece of scrap packing foam (or stacked cardboard). To make the leprechaun head, use the cotton swab to dot pink cheeks onto the third 1½-inch ball. Let all pieces dry.

3 Press the foam head onto the pencil top. Apply a thin layer of glue to a 2-inch piece of toothpick. Insert one end of the toothpick into the top of the foam head, then press on the hat brim and top. Fold the yellow chenille stem in half. One at a time, poke the ends through the black craft foam square, spacing them slightly apart as shown. Pull the stem ends until the fold is flush with the foam square. Trim the excess craft foam around the edges to make the smaller black buckle shape. Wrap the ends of the chenille stem around the hat, twist them at back, then trim the excess. Fold the twisted ends flat to the back of the hat.

4 Cut the orange bump chenille stem to separate the "bumps." Fold one bump in half, then curl the ends to create the mustache. Wrap a scrap piece of chenille stem around the middle of the mustache as shown and insert it into the foam head. Fold the remaining orange "bump" stems in half, then insert into the foam head to make the beard. Cut the 6mm orange chenille stem into 1½-inch to 2-inch lengths, fold in half and insert around the base of the hat for hair. Glue on the wiggle eyes.

What You'll Need

18-inch wood dowel, 5mm

White jumbo loopy chenille

Ruler

Low-temperature glue gun, glue sticks

Poms: 1 white, 2 inches; 2 white, ½ inch each; 1 pink, ¼ inch; 1 white, 1 inch

Scissors

Felt: 3½×5 inches white, 2×2 inches pink

2 wiggle eyes, 10mm each

Tweezers

Black dimensional paint

Small wood teardrop cutout

Paintbrush

Orange acrylic paint

9 inches green yarn

Bunny Plant Poke

Adult help needed

Patterns

teeth

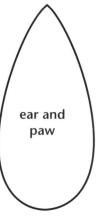
ear and paw

inner ear

1 Spiral-wrap the white chenille around 3 inches of one end of the dowel, spot-gluing every inch.

6

2 For the bunny's head, glue the 2-inch white pom on top of the loopy chenille. To make the cheeks, glue two ½-inch white poms side by side toward the bottom of the head. Using the pattern on page 6, trace and cut out the teeth from the white felt; glue just under the cheeks. For the nose, glue the pink pom to the top middle of the cheeks. Use tweezers to glue 2 wiggle eyes above the cheeks.

3 Using the patterns on page 6, trace and cut out 2 white felt ears, 2 pink felt inner ears, and 2 white felt paws. Glue the inner ears to the white ears; glue to the top of the bunny's head. Glue the 1-inch white pom to the bottom left side of the body for the tail. Make lines on the bunny's paws with black dimensional paint. Let dry. Glue the paws to the bunny's sides, attaching the points at the neck.

4 To make the carrot, paint the wood teardrop orange; let dry. Cut the green yarn into three 3-inch lengths. For the carrot top, align the ends of two lengths of green yarn and tie the third length around the middle of them. Fold the yarn pieces in half, and glue the knot to the back top of the carrot. Glue the carrot to the bunny's left paw. Insert the dowel into a potted plant for a very bunny Easter!

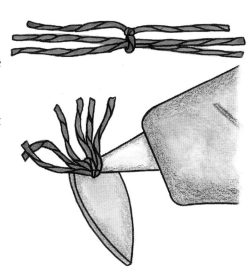

WHAT YOU'LL NEED

Scissors

2×3 inches poster board

Felt: 2×4 inches orange, ¾×1¼ inches red, 1×2 inches purple

Low-temperature glue gun and glue sticks

Orange dimensional paint

2-inch yellow plastic egg

2-inch yellow pom

Yarn: 14 inches yellow, 12 inches green

Ruler

Tweezers

2 wiggle eyes, 10mm each

Craft feathers (assorted colors): three 4 inches long, two 2 inches long

Patterns

Adult help needed

foot

tongue

beak

bow tie

1 Trace and cut out the foot pattern (above). Make 2 feet out of poster board and 2 out of orange felt. Glue 1 felt foot to 1 poster board foot. Squeeze orange dimensional paint lines on the felt foot according to the pattern; let dry. Repeat for the other foot. Position the feet (felt side up) about ¼ inch apart on your work surface. Glue the yellow plastic egg (rounded side) to the feet.

2 To make the egg critter's head, glue the yellow pom to the top of the egg. For hair, cut five 2-inch lengths of yellow yarn, and align the ends. Wrap the remaining 4-inch length of yellow yarn around the middle of the 2-inch lengths; tie a knot. Fold this piece in half; trim the ends to make them even. Glue the knotted end to the top center of the head. Wrap the green yarn around the bottom of the yarn hairs, and tie a bow. Trim the tails.

3 Using the patterns on page 8, trace and cut out the beak from orange felt and the tongue from red felt. Glue the tongue to the inside center of the beak, and fold the beak across the middle as shown on the patterns. Glue the outside of the fold near the bottom of the head. Use tweezers to glue 2 wiggle eyes to the head, just touching the sides of the beak.

4 Use the pattern on page 8 to trace and cut a bow tie from purple felt, and glue it to the egg critter just under the beak. For the tail feathers, glue 4-inch feathers to the lower back of the egg. Glue a 2-inch feather to either side of the body for wings.

Stained Glass Easter Basket

Enlarge pattern
125%

What You'll Need

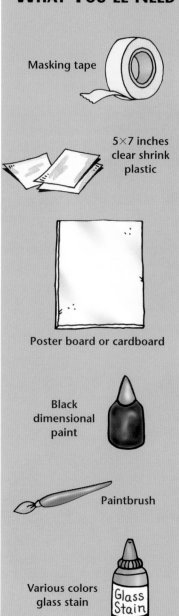

Masking tape

5×7 inches
clear shrink
plastic

Poster board or cardboard

Black
dimensional
paint

Paintbrush

Various colors
glass stain

10

1 Enlarge the pattern on page 10 and copy onto tracing paper. Roll 4 pieces of masking tape into loops with the sticky side out; place them on the 4 corners of the tracing paper without covering any of the pattern. Set the piece of shrink plastic on the pattern with the edges properly aligned, and press down firmly until the tape holds the plastic in place. Place the shrink plastic and pattern on the poster board to protect your work surface.

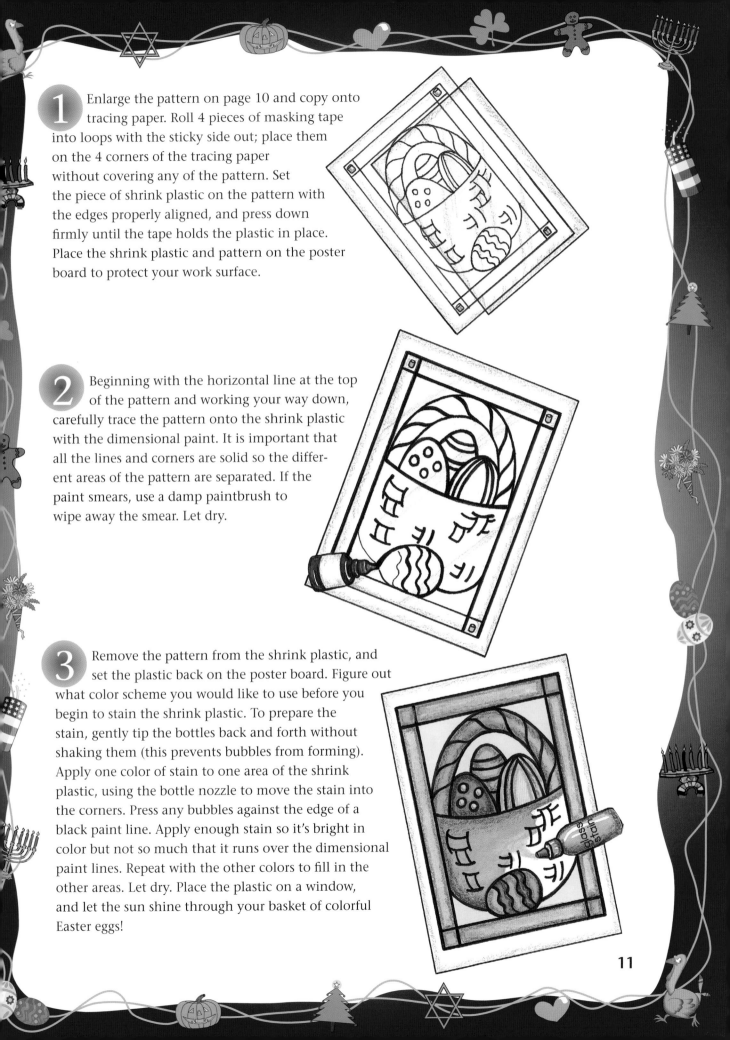

2 Beginning with the horizontal line at the top of the pattern and working your way down, carefully trace the pattern onto the shrink plastic with the dimensional paint. It is important that all the lines and corners are solid so the different areas of the pattern are separated. If the paint smears, use a damp paintbrush to wipe away the smear. Let dry.

3 Remove the pattern from the shrink plastic, and set the plastic back on the poster board. Figure out what color scheme you would like to use before you begin to stain the shrink plastic. To prepare the stain, gently tip the bottles back and forth without shaking them (this prevents bubbles from forming). Apply one color of stain to one area of the shrink plastic, using the bottle nozzle to move the stain into the corners. Press any bubbles against the edge of a black paint line. Apply enough stain so it's bright in color but not so much that it runs over the dimensional paint lines. Repeat with the other colors to fill in the other areas. Let dry. Place the plastic on a window, and let the sun shine through your basket of colorful Easter eggs!

11

What You'll Need

Cardboard tube

Scissors

Ruler

Paint: yellow, orange

Paintbrush

Glue

Wooden skewer

Green tape

Hole punch

Scrap of green craft foam

Tissue paper: yellow, orange

Paper

Markers

Mother's Day Posy

1 Cut seven 1-inch rings from the cardboard tube. Paint 6 yellow and 1 orange. Let dry. Glue the 6 yellow rings around the orange ring, forming a flower.

2 Wrap the skewer in green tape. Punch a hole in the bottom ring of the flower. Slide the skewer into the hole, and glue it in place for a stem. Cut 2 leaves out of green craft foam. Glue them to the stem. Stuff yellow tissue paper into the center of the yellow rings and orange tissue paper into the center of the orange ring. Cut a tag out of paper, fold it over the stem, and glue the ends together. Write your message to Mom on the tag, and decorate it.

Happy Mother's Day

5×7-inch wood plaque

Sandpaper

Soft cloth

Light blue acrylic paint

Paintbrush

Pencil

Bright blue paint pen

Old newspapers

Acrylic spray sealer

3 gold-tone cup hooks, ½ inch each

10 assorted coins, charms, or medallions, between ½ inch and 1½ inches diameter

Low-temperature glue gun, glue sticks

2 soda can tabs

Dad's Key Keeper

Adult help needed

1 Lightly sand the wood plaque; wipe it clean with a soft cloth. Paint the surface with light blue paint. Let dry, then apply a second coat. Let dry.

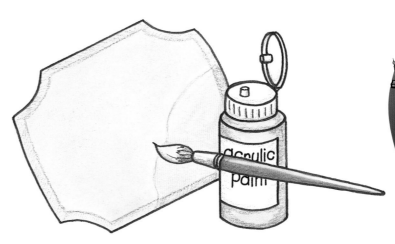

13

2 Using a pencil, lightly print the words "Dad's Keys" on the plaque. Trace the pencil lines with the paint pen. (Hint: Add small dots to the beginning and end of each letter for a fun style.) If the plaque has a raised edge, outline the edge with the paint pen. When you are finished painting, place the plaque outside on old newspapers. Ask an adult to help you lightly spray the plaque with the acrylic spray sealer. Let dry.

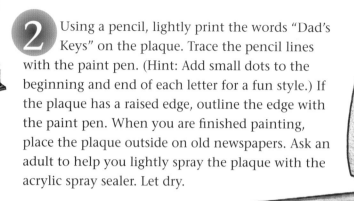

3 Ask an adult to help you screw the 3 cup hooks into the wood, evenly spaced, about 1 inch up from the bottom of the plaque. Arrange the assorted coins, charms, or medallions on the plaque. When you're happy with the design, glue them in place.

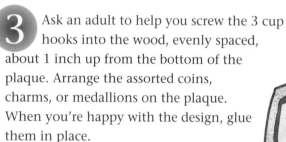

4 To hang the plaque, glue 2 soda can tabs to the back of the plaque so the loops of the tabs will hang on nails in the wall. Give to your dad on Father's Day or any time of year!

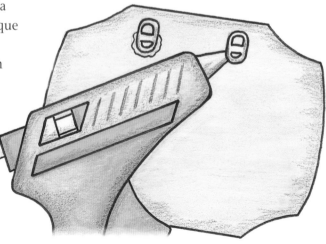

Patriotic Paper Chain

WHAT YOU'LL NEED

Construction paper: red, white, blue

Ruler

Scissors

12-inch dowel

Beads: 2 red, 2⅝ inches each; 2 red, 2⅜ inches each; 2 blue, 2⅜ inches each

Glue stick

18-inch length white satin cord

Star punch

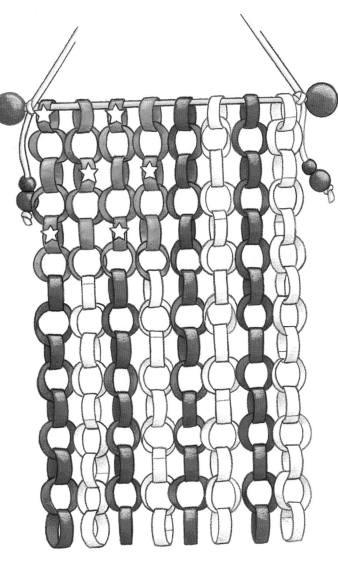

1 Measure and cut paper into ½×4-inch strips. You'll need 50 red, 50 white, and 24 blue. Make 2 paper chains of the red strips, 15 links long. Make 2 paper chains of the white strips, 15 links long. Make 4 paper chains of the blue strips, 6 links long, then add 9 white links to 2 of the blue chains and 9 red links to the other 2 blue chains.

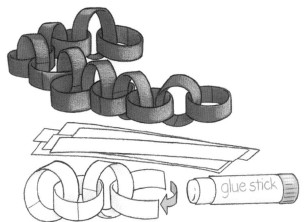

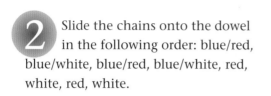

2 Slide the chains onto the dowel in the following order: blue/red, blue/white, blue/red, blue/white, red, white, red, white.

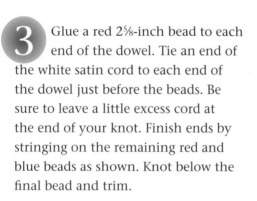

3 Glue a red 2⅝-inch bead to each end of the dowel. Tie an end of the white satin cord to each end of the dowel just before the beads. Be sure to leave a little excess cord at the end of your knot. Finish ends by stringing on the remaining red and blue beads as shown. Knot below the final bead and trim.

4 Punch 6 stars out of white paper and glue to the blue field of your flag. Hang your paper chain on your front door to celebrate the Fourth of July with pride!

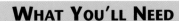

Brown grocery bag (6½×10-inch base, at least 12 inches high)

Ruler

 pencil

Pinking shears

 Scissors

Shiny paper: 9×9 inches white, 9×9 inches orange, 2×3 inches yellow, 2×3 inches green, 2×3 inches black

Glue stick

 Black felt-point permanent marker

Low-temperature glue gun, glue sticks

 1½×18-inch white poster board strip

52-inch length Halloween print craft ribbon, 1½ inches wide

2 sheets black tissue paper

Trick-or-Treat Bag

Adult help needed

1 Use the ruler and pencil to measure and mark the paper bag to 12 inches high. Cut along mark with the pinking shears.

17

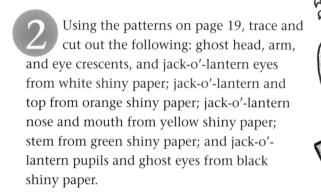

2 Using the patterns on page 19, trace and cut out the following: ghost head, arm, and eye crescents, and jack-o'-lantern eyes from white shiny paper; jack-o'-lantern and top from orange shiny paper; jack-o'-lantern nose and mouth from yellow shiny paper; stem from green shiny paper; and jack-o'-lantern pupils and ghost eyes from black shiny paper.

3 Referring to the illustration, position the parts on your work surface in the following order: ghost head and arm; jack-o'-lantern top, stem, head, eyes, pupils, nose, and mouth; and ghost eyes and eye crescents. Use the glue stick to assemble. Draw the eyebrows and mouth on the ghost and the eyebrows on the pumpkin with the black marker. Use the glue stick to attach the entire jack-o'-lantern/ghost piece to the front of the bag.

4 To make the handle, use a glue gun to attach 1 inch of the poster board strip to the top outside middle of the short side of the bag. Attach the other end of the strip to the other side of the bag. Glue one end of the ribbon to the middle of the bottom of the bag, spot-gluing as you go up the side of the bag, across the poster board strip, down the other side, and across the bottom until the ribbon overlaps the other end. Tuck 2 sheets of black tissue paper inside the bag, and fill it with Halloween treats!

18

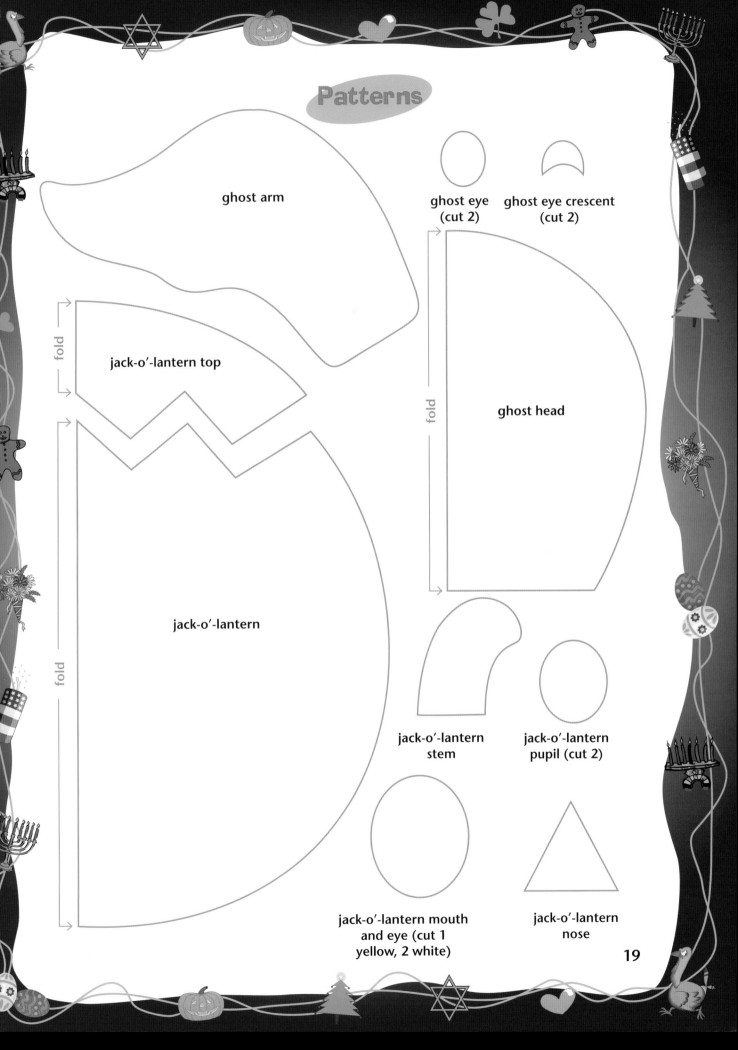

Patterns

ghost arm

ghost eye
(cut 2)

ghost eye crescent
(cut 2)

jack-o'-lantern top

fold

ghost head

fold

jack-o'-lantern

fold

jack-o'-lantern
stem

jack-o'-lantern
pupil (cut 2)

jack-o'-lantern mouth
and eye (cut 1
yellow, 2 white)

jack-o'-lantern
nose

19

Witch's Necklace

Adult help needed

WHAT YOU'LL NEED

8¼×10¾ inches opaque shrink plastic

Medium-point opaque paint markers: black, orange, purple, green

Tape (optional)

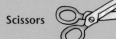
Scissors

Hole punch

Baking sheet

Spatula

30-inch length black rattail cord

Beads: 20 orange pony beads, 6×9mm each; 6 black melon pony beads, 10mm each

1 Using the patterns on page 22, trace the ghost, bat, and witch outlines onto the shrink plastic with the black paint marker. You may want to tape the shrink plastic on top of the patterns to hold the plastic in place.

20

2 Trace the faces and other details from the patterns onto the shapes with the paint markers, using the colors shown. Use a smooth back-and-forth motion when you color so you cover the shrink plastic evenly. Let each color dry completely before adding the next color. (Opaque plastic will appear white when it shrinks, so you don't have to color any areas that should be white.) When the paint is dry, cut out each shape along its outline. Use the hole punch to make 2 holes in each shape as indicated on the patterns.

3 Ask an adult to help you bake the shapes in the oven according to the shrink plastic manufacturer's directions. (Note: Do not remove the shapes from the oven until they have completely flattened. Use a spatula to separate them if the parts stick to each other while baking and to press them after you take them out of the oven.) When the shapes are done baking, remove them from the oven and let them cool.

4 Insert one end of the rattail cord through the holes on the witch's hat, and slide the witch to the middle of the cord. (Hold the two ends of the cord together in one hand and pull on the witch with the other hand to make sure it is in the middle. Keep it in the middle as you work.) Slide 2 orange beads, 1 black bead, and 2 more orange beads onto the cord on the right side of the witch. Slide the ghost onto the cord on the right side of the beads, then add 2 orange beads, 1 black bead, 2 orange beads, 1 black bead, and 2 orange beads onto the cord on the right side of the ghost. Tie a knot in the cord to the right of the last bead.

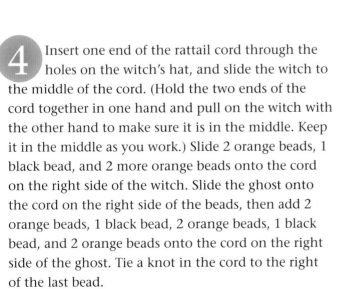

5 Slide 2 orange beads, 1 black bead, and 2 orange beads onto the cord on the left side of the witch. Slide the bat onto the cord on the left side of the beads, then slide 2 orange beads, 1 black bead, 2 orange beads, 1 black bead, and 2 orange beads onto the cord on the left side of the bat. Tie a knot in the cord to the left of the last bead. Tie the ends of the cord together to finish the necklace.

Patterns

WHAT YOU'LL NEED

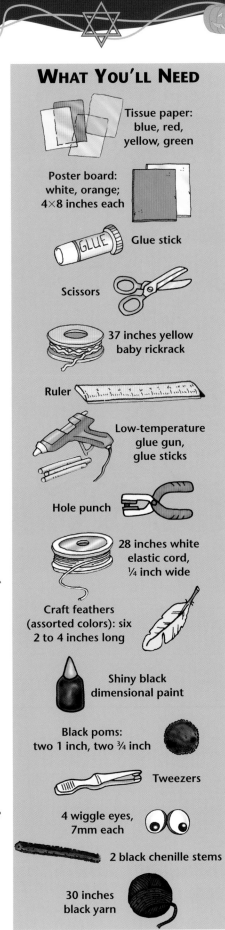

Tissue paper: blue, red, yellow, green

Poster board: white, orange; 4×8 inches each

Glue stick

Scissors

37 inches yellow baby rickrack

Ruler

Low-temperature glue gun, glue sticks

Hole punch

28 inches white elastic cord, ¼ inch wide

Craft feathers (assorted colors): six 2 to 4 inches long

Shiny black dimensional paint

Black poms: two 1 inch, two ¾ inch

Tweezers

4 wiggle eyes, 7mm each

2 black chenille stems

30 inches black yarn

Marvelous Masks

Adult help needed

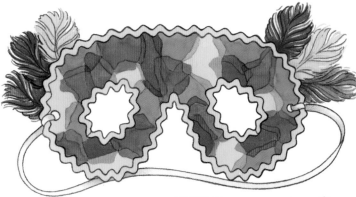

Feather Mask

1 Rip the tissue paper into irregular ½-inch to 1¼-inch pieces. Attach the ripped pieces to the white poster board with the glue stick, overlapping the edges and randomly placing the colors until the entire poster board is covered. Turn over the poster board. Trace and cut out the mask outline and eye holes from the poster board using the pattern on page 24.

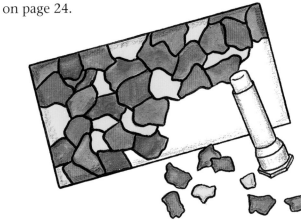

23

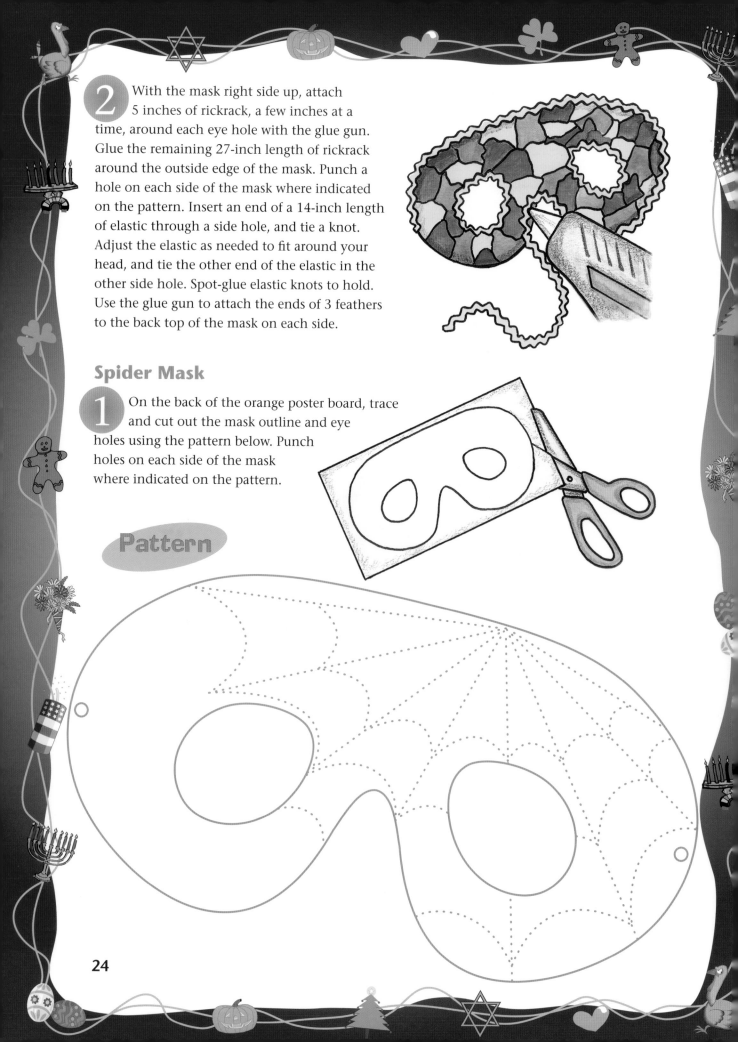

2 With the mask right side up, attach 5 inches of rickrack, a few inches at a time, around each eye hole with the glue gun. Glue the remaining 27-inch length of rickrack around the outside edge of the mask. Punch a hole on each side of the mask where indicated on the pattern. Insert an end of a 14-inch length of elastic through a side hole, and tie a knot. Adjust the elastic as needed to fit around your head, and tie the other end of the elastic in the other side hole. Spot-glue elastic knots to hold. Use the glue gun to attach the ends of 3 feathers to the back top of the mask on each side.

Spider Mask

1 On the back of the orange poster board, trace and cut out the mask outline and eye holes using the pattern below. Punch holes on each side of the mask where indicated on the pattern.

Pattern

2 Lightly draw pencil web guidelines on the front of the mask according to the pattern. Squeeze dimensional paint on the web lines; let dry.

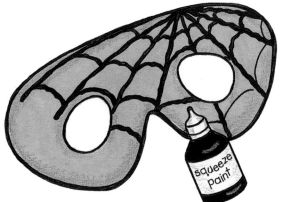

3 Glue a 1-inch and ¾-inch black pom together to make a spider's head and body. Use the tweezers to glue 2 wiggle eyes to the front of the head. For legs, stack and glue the middles of four 3-inch lengths of chenille stems. Glue the body to the top of the leg stack. Bend the end of each leg down ½ inch. Bend out ¼ inch on the end for the foot, and slightly flatten out legs. Repeat to make another spider, but do not flatten out the legs. (This is the hanging spider.)

4 Leaving 2 inches unglued, begin gluing a 22-inch length of yarn above the left hole punch, continuing all the way around the outside of the mask. Glue the dangling end of yarn between the hanging spider's head and body poms. Cut the remaining length of yarn in half, and glue each length around an eye hole. Glue the second spider to the upper right side of the mask. Attach the elastic cord as explained in step 2 of the Feather Mask.

Spooky Tic-Tac-Toe

WHAT YOU'LL NEED

Scissors

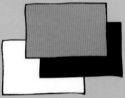
Magnetic sheeting:
1½×7½ inches orange,
1½×7½ inches white,
5×5 inches black

Manicure scissors
(optional)

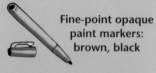
Fine-point opaque
paint markers:
brown, black

20 inches green
satin ribbon,
⅛ inch wide

Ruler

Glue

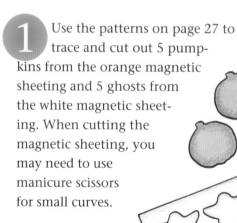

1. Use the patterns on page 27 to trace and cut out 5 pumpkins from the orange magnetic sheeting and 5 ghosts from the white magnetic sheeting. When cutting the magnetic sheeting, you may need to use manicure scissors for small curves.

Patterns

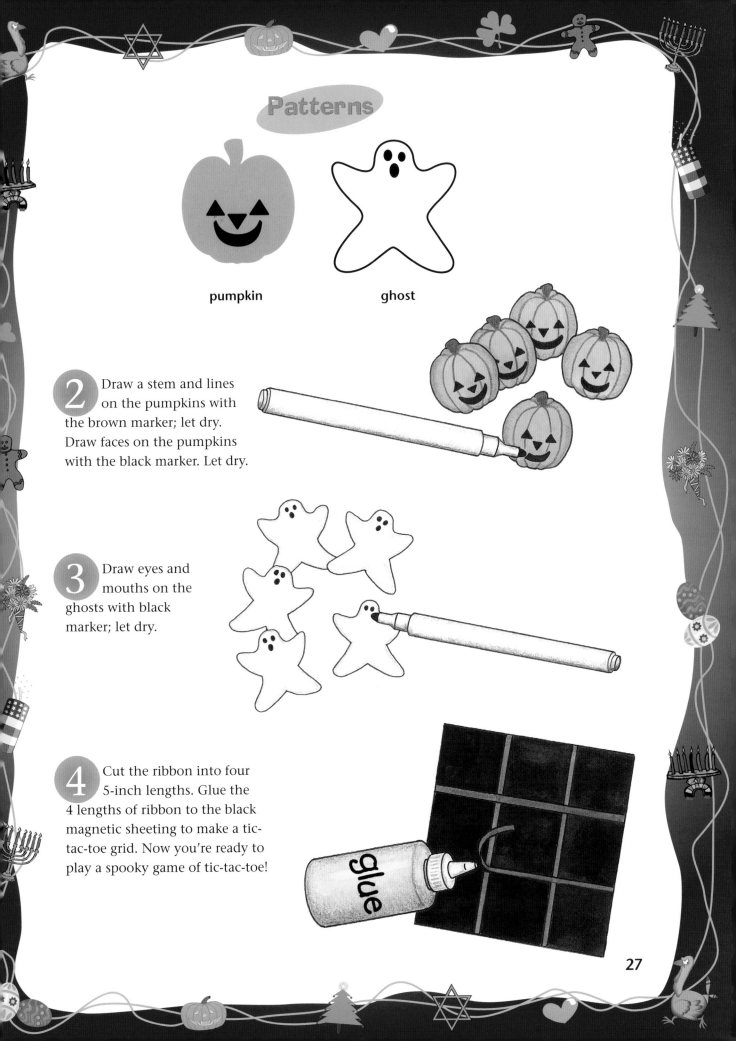

pumpkin

ghost

2 Draw a stem and lines on the pumpkins with the brown marker; let dry. Draw faces on the pumpkins with the black marker. Let dry.

3 Draw eyes and mouths on the ghosts with black marker; let dry.

4 Cut the ribbon into four 5-inch lengths. Glue the 4 lengths of ribbon to the black magnetic sheeting to make a tic-tac-toe grid. Now you're ready to play a spooky game of tic-tac-toe!

glue

Happy Turkey Banner

WHAT YOU'LL NEED

Scissors

Cardstock: two 8½×11 inches light brown, goldenrod; scrap red

16 craft feathers (assorted colors), 4 inches long

Tacky glue

Black felt-point permanent marker

20-inch length red ribbon, 1 inch wide

1 Use the patterns on page 30 to trace and cut out the following: turkey body, wings, and head from light brown cardstock, beak and legs from goldenrod cardstock, and wattle from red cardstock.

2 Arrange the craft feathers in a fan shape (alternating colors) on an 8½×11 inch sheet of light brown cardstock. Check the placement of the feathers on the sheet by placing the turkey body over the bottoms of the feathers. The bottom of the body should align with the bottom of the cardstock, and the top of the body should cover the feather ends. Adjust the feathers as needed. Set the turkey body aside, and secure feathers with glue. Glue head and wings to turkey body. Use a black marker to draw eyes on the turkey head and wing lines on the wings.

3 Glue the turkey body down to cover the bottom of the feathers. Glue turkey legs to body. Glue beak and red wattle on the turkey head. Trim excess light brown cardstock below the wings.

4 Cut an 8½×6 inch piece of goldenrod cardstock, and fold in half lengthwise. Glue half of the folded paper to the back side of the banner top as shown, and glue the other half to the front of the banner. (Do not glue goldenrod cardstock to itself.) Let glue dry. Write "Happy Thanks-giving" on the top with a black marker. Thread the red ribbon through the folded cardstock and tie to create a hanger.

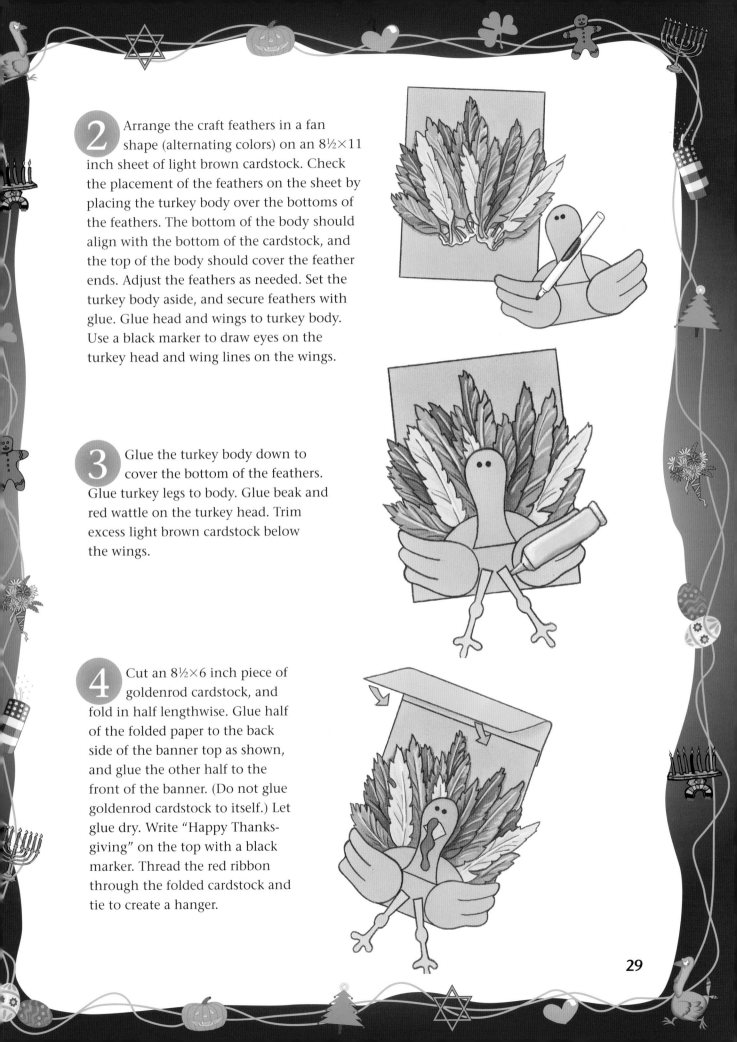

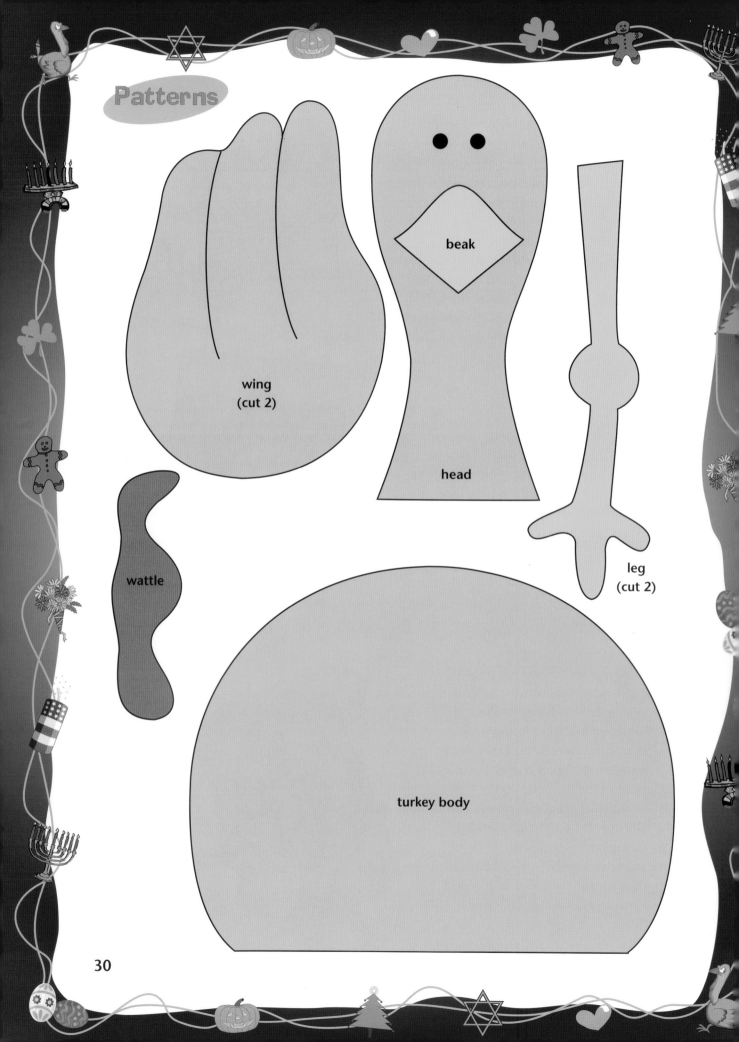

Patterns

wing
(cut 2)

beak

head

leg
(cut 2)

wattle

turkey body

30

WHAT YOU'LL NEED

Scissors

Cardstock: dark red, dark orange, red, mustard, dark brown, tan

GLUE Glue stick

Wiggle eyes

Pencil

Lightbulb slip cover

Brown marker

Ruler

Brown yarn

Tom the Turkey Wants You

1 Use the patterns on page 33 to trace and cut out the following: head, body, neck, and 2 feathers from dark red cardstock; legs, hair, 2 wings (use the feather pattern), and 2 feathers from dark orange cardstock; beak, wattle, and feet from red cardstock; 4 feathers from mustard cardstock.

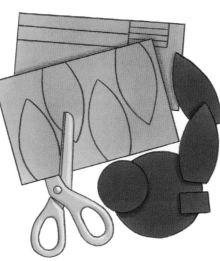

2 Attach the turkey neck to the body and head with the glue stick. Add eyes, beak, and wattle to the head. Add wings to the body.

3 Make a small ¼-inch fold in the middle of each leg. Use the glue stick to attach a foot to the bottom of each leg. Attach the legs to the bottom of the body. Curl the paper strips for the hair by wrapping each strip around the pencil. Glue the curled hair to the back of the turkey head. Add the feathers to the back of the turkey body using the glue stick. Arrange the feathers in a fan shape, alternating colors.

5 Apply glue generously to the back side of the turkey starting at half of the neck and working down to the body. Add glue to the bottom of each feather and to the wings. Attach the turkey to the box. The legs should dangle.

4 Using the lightbulb cover as a template, measure and cut 2 pieces of dark brown cardstock for the front and back of the box. Measure and cut 2 pieces of cardstock (use any cardstock left over) for the sides. Cut another piece that is wide enough to cover the bottom plus ½ inch on each side. Glue this piece to the bottom first, folding ½ inch up to each side. Use the glue stick to adhere the side pieces and then the front and back pieces to the cover. Trim if needed.

6 Cut an 8½×2½-inch rectangle from tan cardstock. Fold the card in half. With the brown marker write "I am thankful for...," on the front of the card. Cut approximately 12 inches of yarn. Place one end of the yarn through the inside of the card, and tie a bow. Place the card inside the box. Repeat steps to make additional cards. At Thanksgiving dinner, ask everyone to fill out a card and put it in the box. Take turns reading each other's cards for a special way to put the "thanks" in "Thanksgiving"!

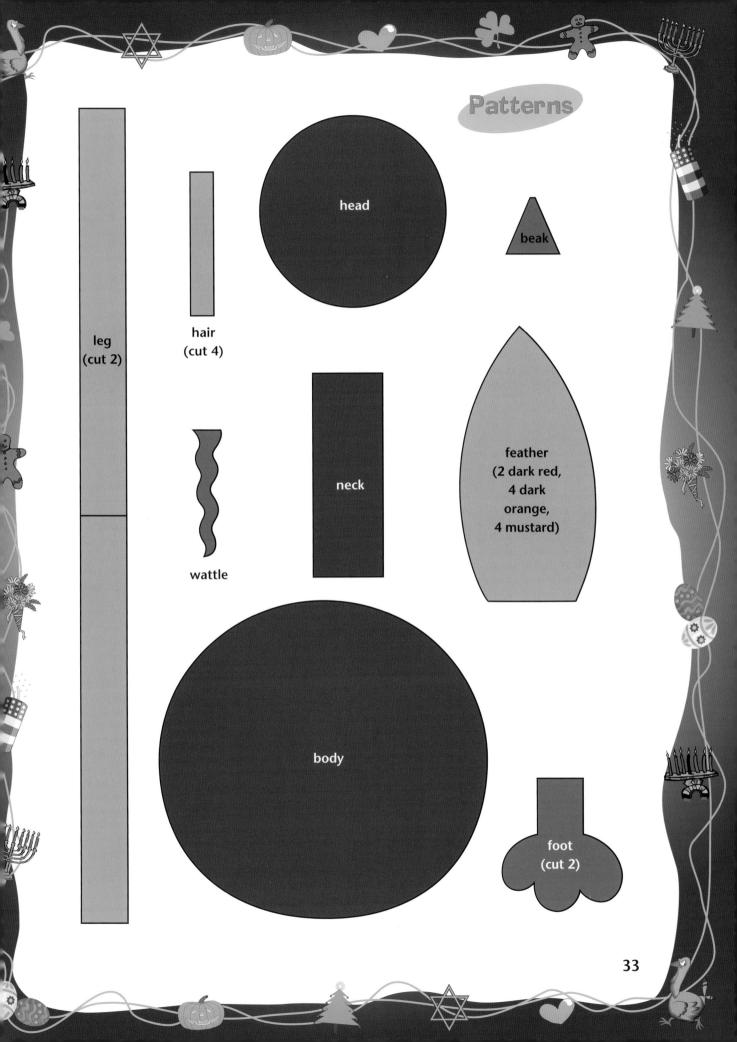

Patterns

leg
(cut 2)

hair
(cut 4)

head

beak

wattle

neck

feather
(2 dark red,
4 dark
orange,
4 mustard)

body

foot
(cut 2)

33

Happy Hanukkah Paper

WHAT YOU'LL NEED

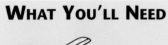 Scissors

 Compressed sponge

 Paper towels

 Kraft paper

  Acrylic paint: blue, yellow, white

 3 foam plates

 Old toothbrush

Patterns

Star of David   dreidel

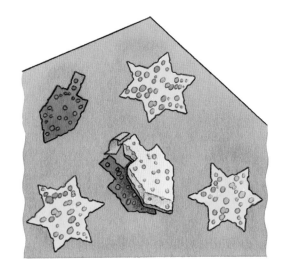

1 Use the patterns on page 34 to trace and cut out a dreidel and Star of David shape from the compressed sponge. Run the sponge shapes under water, and press out any excess water with paper towels.

3 Use the dreidel sponge and blue paint to sponge dreidels on your gift wrap. Let dry.

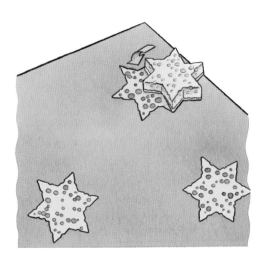

2 Measure and cut the kraft paper to the size of the gift you need to wrap. Pour blue and yellow paint onto foam plates. Dip the Star of David sponge into yellow paint, coating one side. Press the sponge onto the paper. Make as many stars as you'd like, but leave room for dreidels. (You will probably have to dip the sponge into the paint a few times to cover the paper with stars.) Let dry.

4 Pour the white paint onto a foam plate, then load an old toothbrush with the paint. To spatter-paint the paper, hold the brush over the paper and run your finger over the bristles. Let dry. Wrap a Hanukkah gift with the paper, and add a matching ribbon for that extra-special touch!

Star of David Coasters

What You'll Need

18 craft sticks

Markers

Scissors

Scrap cardstock or cardboard

Craft foam: orange, purple, yellow

Heavy craft glue or hot glue

Glitter glue

Pattern

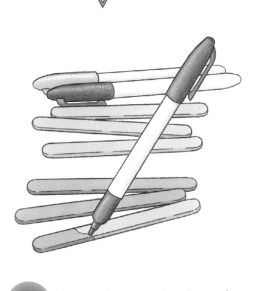

1 Use markers to color the craft sticks. Color 6 green, 6 blue, and 6 yellow.

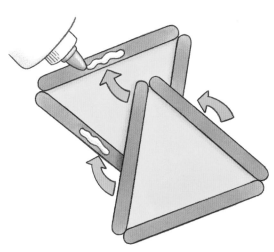

3 Glue 3 blue craft sticks to the edges of a piece of yellow craft foam so that they form a triangle. Repeat for remaining blue craft sticks and foam. Add glue to one craft stick triangle. Attach another craft stick triangle as shown to form a coaster. Repeat with the green craft sticks and orange foam and with the yellow craft sticks and purple foam.

2 Trace the pattern on page 36 onto scrap cardstock or cardboard and cut out. Use this template to cut out 2 pieces of orange craft foam, 2 pieces of purple craft foam, and 2 pieces of yellow craft foam.

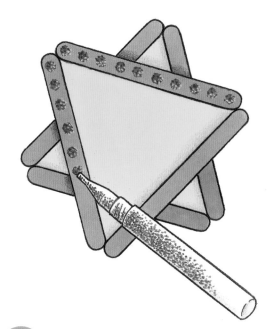

4 Add glitter glue to decorate the coasters, then set them aside to dry.

37

Candy Cane Doorknob Decoration

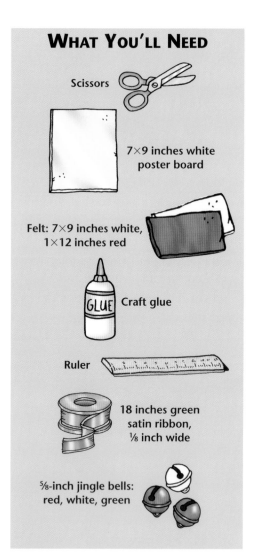

WHAT YOU'LL NEED

Scissors

7×9 inches white poster board

Felt: 7×9 inches white, 1×12 inches red

GLUE — Craft glue

Ruler

18 inches green satin ribbon, ⅛ inch wide

⅝-inch jingle bells: red, white, green

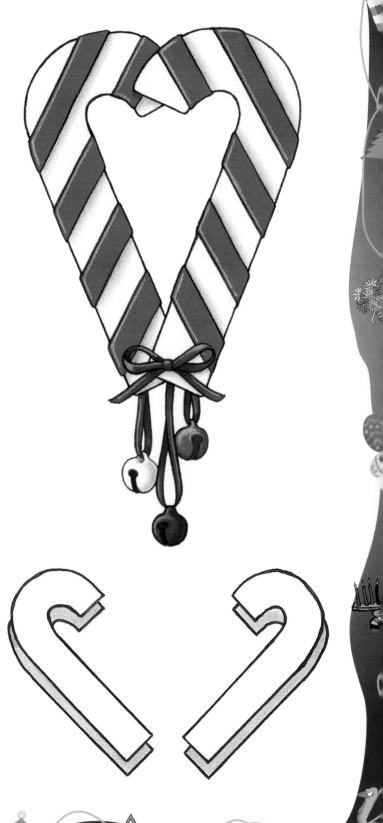

1 Use the pattern on page 39 to trace and cut out 4 candy canes—2 from poster board and 2 from white felt. Lay the poster board canes on your work surface so the top curves face the center. Starting on the left side, glue one felt cane to each poster board cane.

38

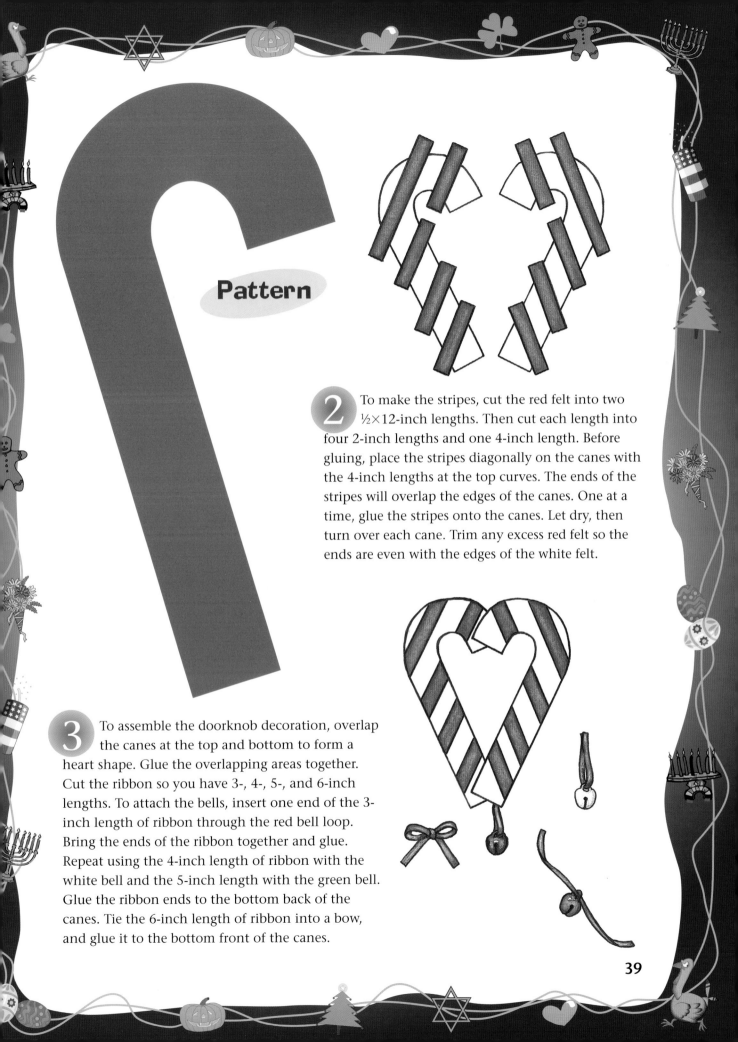

Pattern

2 To make the stripes, cut the red felt into two ½×12-inch lengths. Then cut each length into four 2-inch lengths and one 4-inch length. Before gluing, place the stripes diagonally on the canes with the 4-inch lengths at the top curves. The ends of the stripes will overlap the edges of the canes. One at a time, glue the stripes onto the canes. Let dry, then turn over each cane. Trim any excess red felt so the ends are even with the edges of the white felt.

3 To assemble the doorknob decoration, overlap the canes at the top and bottom to form a heart shape. Glue the overlapping areas together. Cut the ribbon so you have 3-, 4-, 5-, and 6-inch lengths. To attach the bells, insert one end of the 3-inch length of ribbon through the red bell loop. Bring the ends of the ribbon together and glue. Repeat using the 4-inch length of ribbon with the white bell and the 5-inch length with the green bell. Glue the ribbon ends to the bottom back of the canes. Tie the 6-inch length of ribbon into a bow, and glue it to the bottom front of the canes.

Christmas Card Star

WHAT YOU'LL NEED

Christmas cards

Scissors

8×16 inches white poster board

Craft glue

Hole punch

Glittering gold dimensional paint

8-inch length green satin ribbon, ⅛-inch wide

Pattern

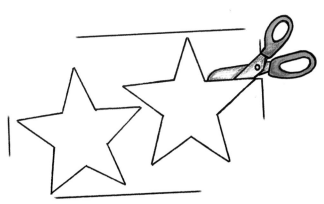

1. Find designs and figures you like on old Christmas cards. The shapes can be irregular along the edges. They don't have to be exact because trimming will be done later. Cut out the shapes, and set them aside. Use the star pattern on page 40 to trace and cut out 2 stars from the poster board.

3. Glue the star that is completely covered to the top center of the star with the blank center, staggering the points as shown. Squeeze dimensional paint around all the edges; let dry.

2. Glue the Christmas card shapes to one star, overlapping card edges and allowing cards to extend beyond the star edges. Put your favorite picture in the center. (You should have a good number of card shapes left over for the second star.) When the star is covered, trim the card shape even with the star edges. Punch a hole near each point of the star. Leaving the center uncovered, repeat this step to cover just the points of the other star.

4. To make the hanger loop, insert one end of the green satin ribbon through a hole. Bring the ends together, and tie a knot. If you plan on hanging the star in a window or on a tree, you may choose to decorate both sides (in step 2).

Christmas Tree Shirt

Adult help needed

WHAT YOU'LL NEED

 Scissors

 Felt: 6×8 inches green; brown scrap

 Low-temperature glue gun, glue sticks

21-inch length flat white lace, ½ inch wide

 Faux gems: 16 assorted, 1 star

 Repositionable glue

 Paintbrush

 White sweatshirt

1️⃣ Use the pattern on page 43 to trace and cut out the tree from green felt. Cut a small tree trunk out of brown felt.

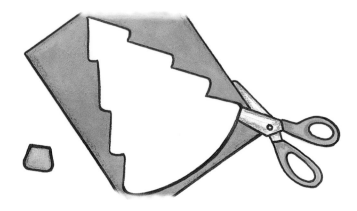

42

2 Glue the edge of the trunk under the bottom center of the tree so the tree overlaps the trunk about ½ inch. For the tree garland, use the glue gun to attach one end of the lace to the top left of the tree. Drape the lace back and forth across the tree, folding over and gluing the lace each time it changes direction. When needed, add a spot of glue to any curves to keep the lace flat against the felt. Use the glue gun to randomly attach the gems to the tree. Glue the star gem at the top.

3 Turn the tree over and apply 2 or 3 coats of the repositionable glue according to the manufacturer's instructions. Let the glue dry for 24 hours, then attach the tree to the front of the sweatshirt. Remove the tree before washing.

Pattern

Try This!
Don't want a Christmas tree shirt? No problem! Just make a different shape out of felt, and follow the instructions above to attach it to your sweatshirt.

WHAT YOU'LL NEED

Scissors

Sandpaper

2 sheets opaque shrink plastic, 8¼×10¾ inches each

Black medium-point permanent marker

Acrylic paint: pink, light brown

Paintbrushes

Hole punch

Cookie sheet

Aluminum foil

34 inches white baby rickrack

Ruler

Craft glue

Tweezers

4 wiggle eyes, 7mm

1×1 inches green felt

3 red buttons, ⅛ inch each

2-inch length green eyelet lace, 1 inch wide

22 inches red satin ribbon, ⅛ inch wide

Gingerbread Kid Ornaments

Adult help needed

1 Trace and cut out the gingerbread pattern on page 46. Lightly sand both sheets of shrink plastic, then trace the pattern on each sheet with the marker. Paint pink circles for the cheeks, then paint the rest of the shape with a thin coat of light brown; let dry. Cut out each shape. Punch a hole in each, ½ inch down from the top of the head. Place the cutouts on a foil-covered cookie sheet, then follow the manufacturer's instructions for baking. Let cool.

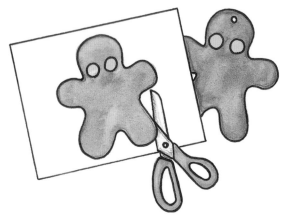

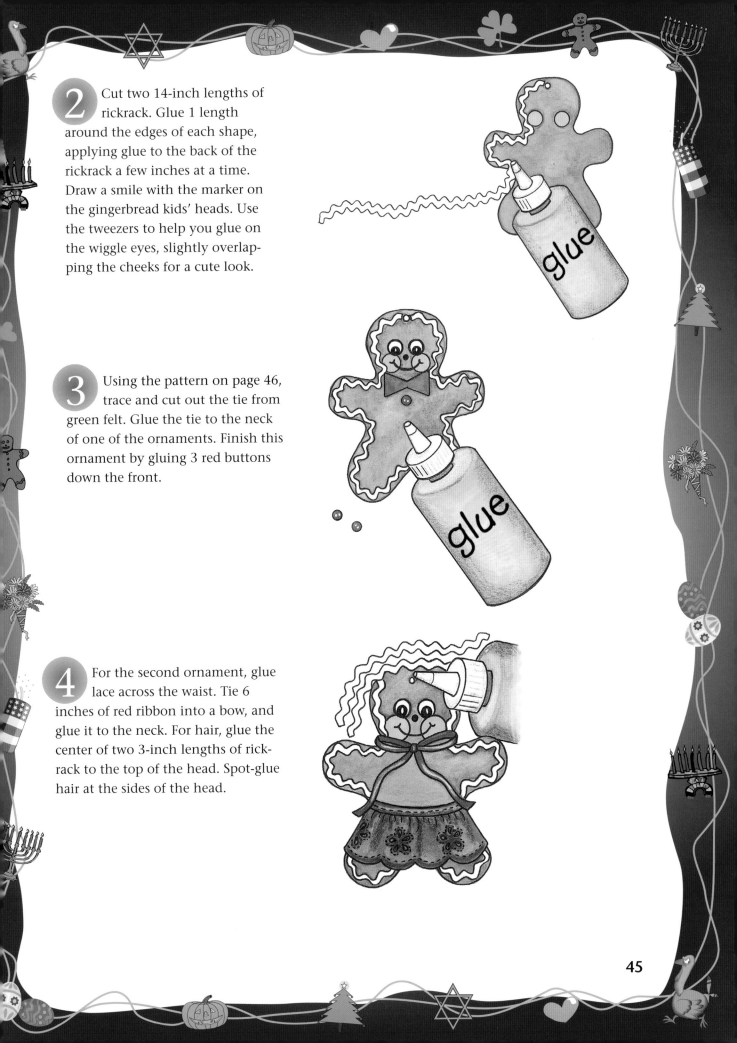

2 Cut two 14-inch lengths of rickrack. Glue 1 length around the edges of each shape, applying glue to the back of the rickrack a few inches at a time. Draw a smile with the marker on the gingerbread kids' heads. Use the tweezers to help you glue on the wiggle eyes, slightly overlapping the cheeks for a cute look.

3 Using the pattern on page 46, trace and cut out the tie from green felt. Glue the tie to the neck of one of the ornaments. Finish this ornament by gluing 3 red buttons down the front.

4 For the second ornament, glue lace across the waist. Tie 6 inches of red ribbon into a bow, and glue it to the neck. For hair, glue the center of two 3-inch lengths of rickrack to the top of the head. Spot-glue hair at the sides of the head.

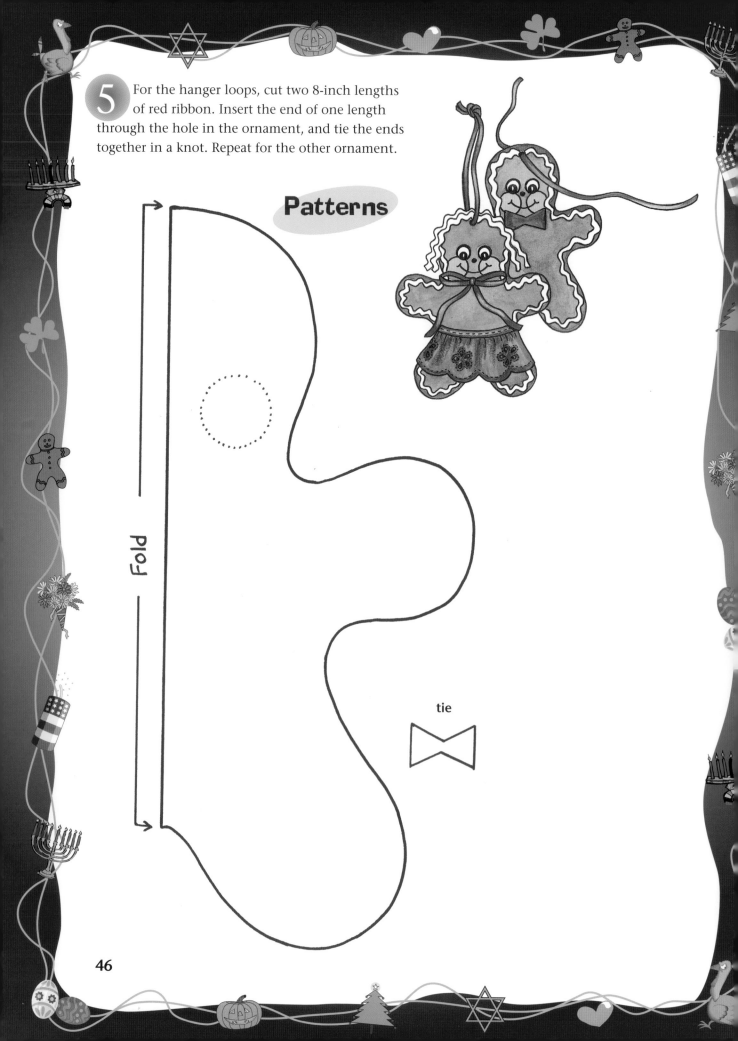

5 For the hanger loops, cut two 8-inch lengths of red ribbon. Insert the end of one length through the hole in the ornament, and tie the ends together in a knot. Repeat for the other ornament.

Patterns

Fold

tie

WHAT YOU'LL NEED

Scissors

Green poster board

Craft knife

Red plastic tape, ¾ inch wide

Ruler

Hole punch

Craft glue

Glitter

8½×11-inch sheet white paper

Red construction paper

Shiny red and white gift wrap

Adult help needed

Paper Cornucopia

1. Use the pattern on page 48 to trace and cut out the triangle shape. Trace the triangle onto the green poster board 4 times, repositioning it as shown below. Cut out the shape along the outer lines only.

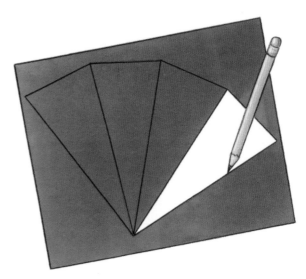

Pattern

2 Ask an adult to help you score the 3 interior lines with the craft knife. Bend the poster board along the scored lines.

3 Cut three 6½-inch pieces of plastic tape. Have an adult help you use the ruler and craft knife to cut the pieces in half lengthwise (making six ⅜-inch-wide strips). Tape the 2 cut edges of the poster board together, taking care to center the tape along the edge. Trim the excess tape at the bottom and top edges of the cone. Tape the other 3 edges of the cone. Use the remaining strips to tape around the top edge of the cone.

4 Punch a hole in opposite sides of the cone. Fold a 12-inch length of plastic tape lengthwise, sticky sides together, to make a hanging ribbon. Insert 1 end of the ribbon in each of the holes, and tie an overhand knot on each end inside the cone. Make a long squiggle of craft glue on 1 side of the cone. Sprinkle glitter on the glue, then gently knock off the excess glitter. Let dry completely.

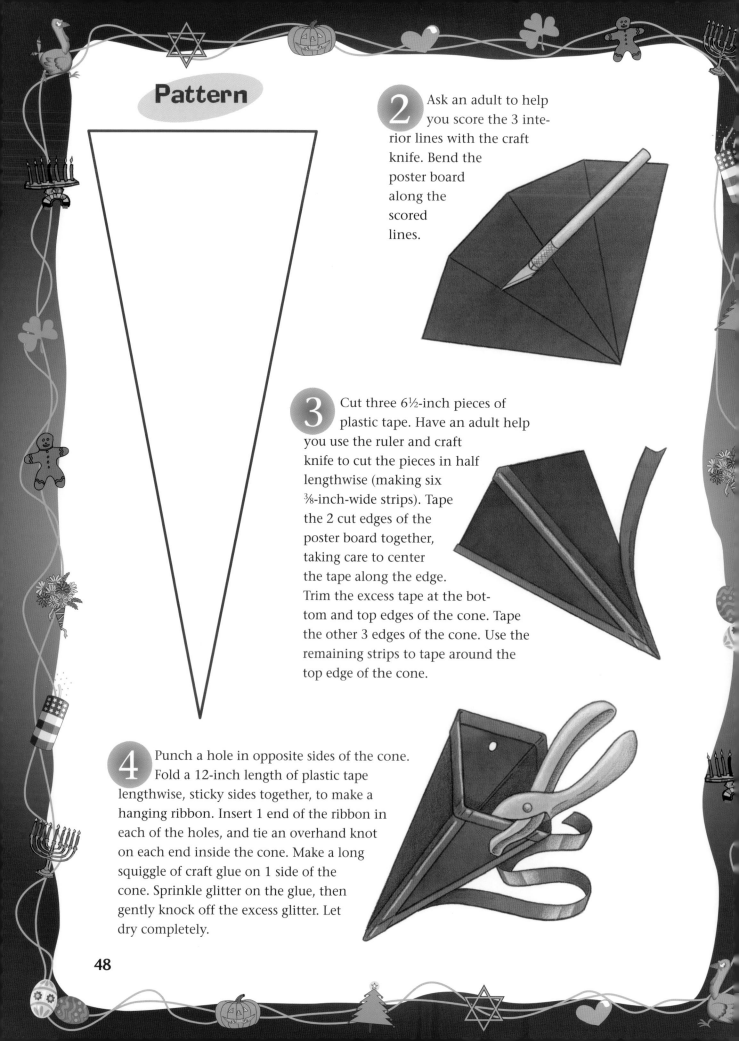

Pleated Fan

1 Fold the white paper in half along its length. Cut along the crease line to make two 8½×5½-inch rectangles. With 1 rectangle, pleat the paper by accordion-folding it, back and forth, in ¼-inch folds. Cut off the last fold with scissors if it is less than the full width.

2 Bunching the folds together, cut one end of the pleated paper at an angle. Make a series of small triangular cuts along both sides of the pleats.

3 Cut two ¼-inch-wide strips from the red construction paper, one 3 inches long, the other 6 inches long. Glue the ends of the longer strip to each side of the uncut end of the pleated paper to make a hanging loop. Glue the shorter strip around the base of the loop; trim excess. Spread out the pleats.

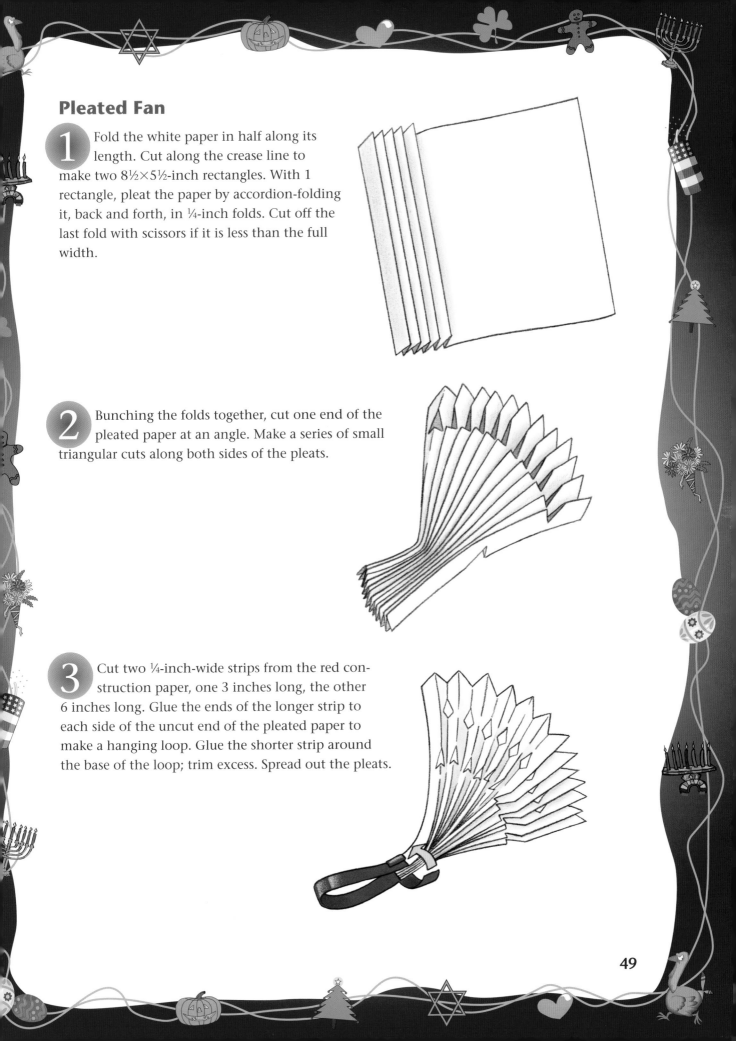

Scandinavian Heart Basket

1 Measure and cut a 3×9-inch rectangle out of both the red and the white gift wrap. Fold the red rectangle in half so the short ends meet. At the folded edge, measure and cut 2 lines that are 1 inch apart and 3⅛ inches long. Round the opposite corners. Repeat for the white rectangle.

2 Open up the top red strip and insert the top white strip between the layers. Then insert the red strip between the layers of the middle white strip. Insert the bottom white strip between the layers of the red strip. The middle red strip is woven between the top white, over the middle white, and between the bottom white strips. The bottom red strip is woven the same as the top red strip.

3 Cut a ½-inch-wide handle from the red gift wrap. Fold it in half, and glue the ends to the inside of the basket.

Stamped Gift Bag

WHAT YOU'LL NEED

Scissors

Christmas card (old or new) with "Merry Christmas" or other holiday greeting

White bakery bag (3¾×5½-inch base, at least 11 inches high)

Holiday rubber stamps

Red or green ink pad (or any color that coordinates with card)

Paper

Paper towels

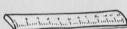
Craft glue

Clear tape

Ruler

Hole punch

24-inch length red rattail cord

Jingle bells, ⅝-inch: 1 red, 1 green

2 sheets tissue paper (any color that coordinates with card and stamping ink)

1. Carefully cut out a message from a Christmas greeting card, leaving between ⅛- and ¼-inch trim around the outside edge of the letters. Plan where you are going to place the message on the bakery bag, but do not glue it on yet.

51

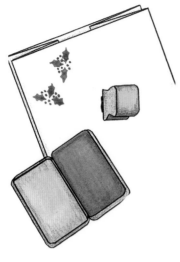

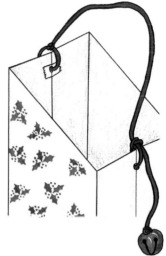

2 One at a time, gently press the rubber stamps onto the ink pad. Remove and press them onto a sheet of scrap paper to practice stamping. When ready, stamp the designs on the flat bag around where the message will be located. Glue the message onto the bag. (Use a damp paper towel to clean the rubber stamps before changing colors and when you are finished.)

4 To make the handle, paper punch one hole through each piece of tape you just applied. Insert 1 end of the rattail cord through the inside of the bag and out the hole. Thread a jingle bell on the same end. Tie a knot on the end to hold the bell. Tie another knot about 2½ inches up through the hole and around the top of the bag to keep the handle from slipping. Repeat to attach the cord to the other side.

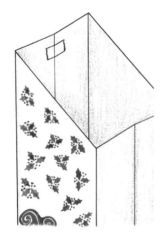

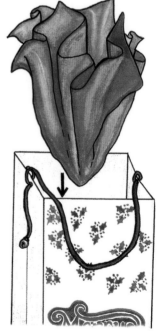

3 Before punching the holes for the handles, reinforce the area by placing a small piece of clear tape inside a narrow side of the bag, centered and about ½-inch down from the top edge. Repeat on the other narrow side of the bag.

5 After placing the gift in the bag, you'll be ready to finish the project with this last step. To tuck the tissue paper into the bag, open each sheet and lay it flat on the work area. Layer the paper, making one sheet crisscross over the other. Grasp the center of the pile and pull up to gather. (Be careful not to tear the tissue.) Push the gathers into the bag, and arrange the tissue paper at the top.

Santa Claus Stocking

Adult help needed

Using the patterns on pages 55 and 56

What You'll Need

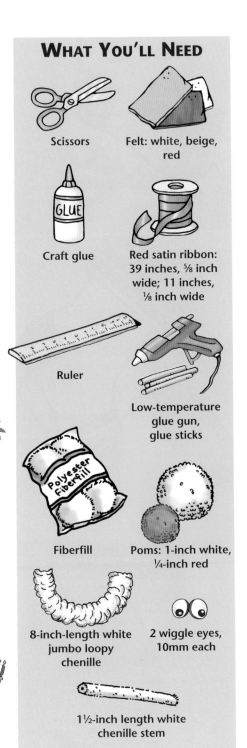

Scissors

Felt: white, beige, red

Craft glue

Red satin ribbon: 39 inches, ⅝ inch wide; 11 inches, ⅛ inch wide

Ruler

Low-temperature glue gun, glue sticks

Fiberfill

Poms: 1-inch white, ¼-inch red

8-inch-length white jumbo loopy chenille

2 wiggle eyes, 10mm each

1½-inch length white chenille stem

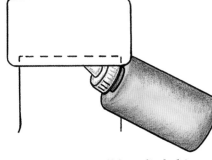

1 Using the patterns on pages 55 and 56, trace and cut the stocking foot and cuff from white felt to make the front. Apply craft glue to the top edge of the stocking. Attach the cuff so that the bottom edge overlaps the top of the stocking by about ¼ inch. Allow the glue to dry. Cut three 6-inch lengths of the ⅝-inch ribbon. Lay the stripes side by side across the cuff, allowing an even amount of white space above, below, and in between each red stripe. (The stripes will be a little bit longer than the cuff. Let the extra length hang over the edge of the cuff for now.) Apply craft glue to the back of each ribbon length, and attach them to the cuff. After the glue has dried, trim the ribbon ends so they are even with the cuff.

2 For the heel, use three 3-inch lengths of the ⅝-inch ribbon. Glue and trim the ribbon as shown on the pattern. Cut a 3-inch length of the ⅛-inch ribbon. Glue it across the top of the heel ribbons to cover the ends. After the glue has dried, trim the ribbon end so it is even with the felt heel. For the toe, cut three 4-inch lengths of the ⅝-inch ribbon. Position the ribbon diagonally on the toe as shown on the pattern. Glue and trim these stripes the same way you did on the cuff.

3 Using the patterns on pages 55 and 56, trace and cut another stocking foot and cuff from white felt to make the back. Glue them together as in Step 1, making sure the toe is pointed in the opposite direction of your stocking front. Align the front and back halves, one on top of the other. Lift up the stocking front and apply a line of glue ⅛ inch in from the edge of the stocking, leaving the top open. Realign the back and the front, and let dry. Make the hanger loop by gluing together the ends of an 8-inch length of ⅛-inch ribbon. Insert the ends between the cuff layers on the top right side and glue.

4 Using the patterns on page 55, trace and cut the face from beige felt, the hat and the mouth from red felt, and the mustache from white felt. To assemble, use the glue gun. For the hat, roll the red felt into a cone shape, slightly overlapping the straight sides. Glue the overlap area together. Position and glue the top of the face inside the hat. Glue the face and the lower back of the hat to the stocking. Apply glue to the lower front edge of the hat, and glue on the fiberfill. Fold over the tip of the hat, and glue it to the stocking. Glue the white pom on the tip of the hat.

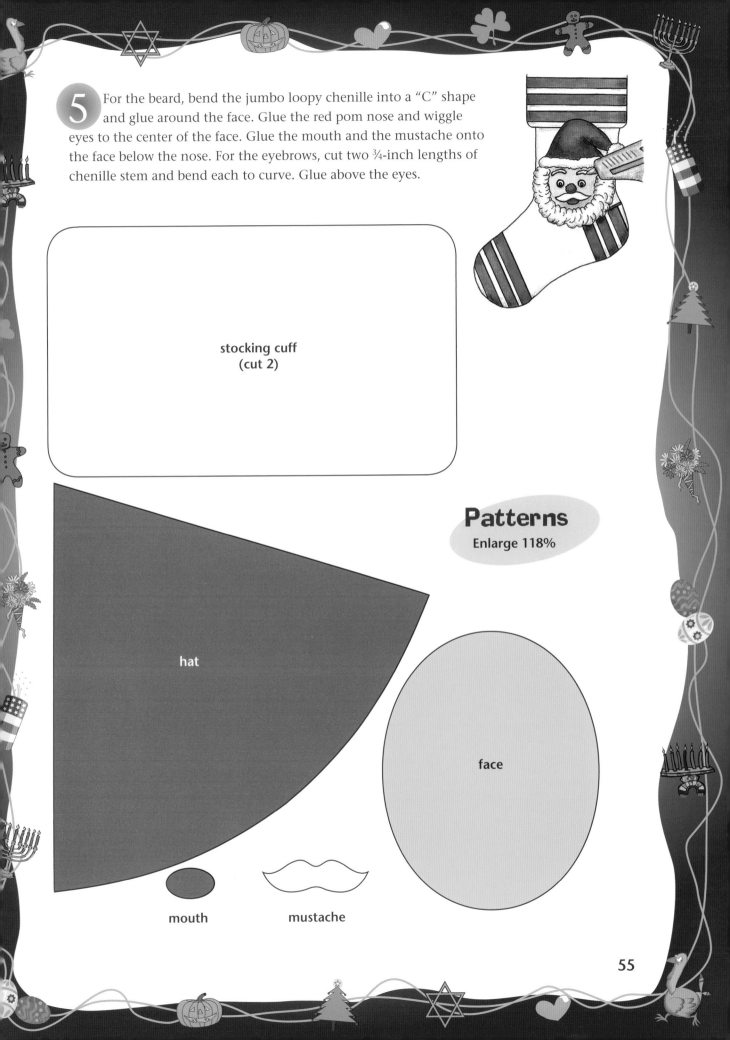

5 For the beard, bend the jumbo loopy chenille into a "C" shape and glue around the face. Glue the red pom nose and wiggle eyes to the center of the face. Glue the mouth and the mustache onto the face below the nose. For the eyebrows, cut two ¾-inch lengths of chenille stem and bend each to curve. Glue above the eyes.

stocking cuff
(cut 2)

Patterns
Enlarge 118%

hat

face

mouth

mustache

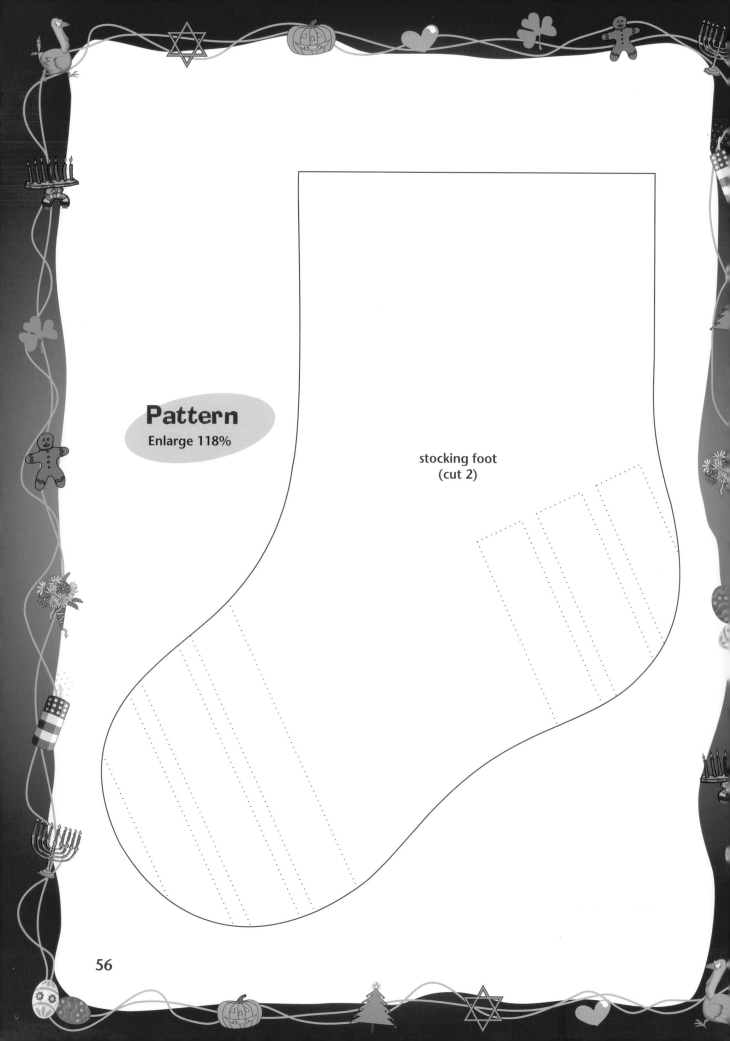

Pattern
Enlarge 118%

stocking foot
(cut 2)

Kwanzaa Calendar

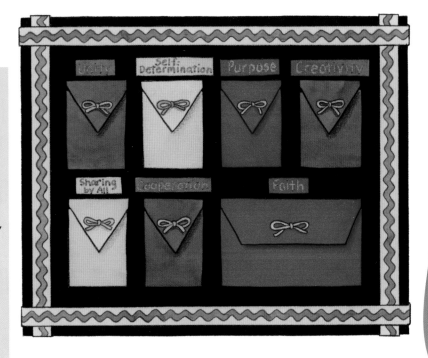

WHAT YOU'LL NEED

Felt: 8×11 inches green, 8×8 inches yellow, 8×11 inches red, 16×20 inches black

Ruler

 Scissors

 Glittering gold dimensional paint

 2 yards and 4 inches yellow satin ribbon, 1 inch wide

 Craft glue

 2 yards and 4 inches jumbo bright green rickrack

1 yard and 14 inches gold metallic cord

① Cut 3 green, 2 yellow, and 2 red 1×5-inch pieces of felt. Carefully write the following words on the felt with dimensional paint (you may want to lightly write the words first in pencil): Unity, Self-Determination, Purpose, Creativity, Sharing by All, Cooperation, and Faith. Let the paint dry, then trim the ends of the felt pieces to within ¼ inch of the words.

2 Cut the ribbon into two 17-inch lengths and two 21-inch lengths. Glue the 17-inch lengths of ribbon vertically on the black felt, ½ inch from the sides. Cut two 17-inch lengths of rickrack, and glue them on top of each 17-inch length of ribbon. Fold over and glue the ends of the 17-inch pieces of ribbon and rickrack to the back of the black felt. Glue the two 21-inch lengths of ribbon horizontally on the black felt, ½ inch from the top and bottom. Cut two 21-inch lengths of rickrack and glue 1 on top of each 21-inch length of ribbon. Fold and glue the ends of the 21-inch pieces of ribbon and rickrack to the back of the black felt.

3 Using the patterns on page 59, trace and cut out pockets and flaps from the felt as follows: 3 small each from green, 2 small each from yellow, 1 small and 1 large each from red.

4 Arrange the pockets, flaps, and words on the black felt as shown. To glue the pockets to the black felt, glue the bottom of each pocket first, then slightly push in the sides of the pocket and glue them. (This will loosen the pockets to allow space for gifts.) Glue the top edge of the flaps about ¼ inch above the pockets. Finally, glue the words above the flaps.

58

5 Cut seven 6-inch lengths of gold cord. Tie a bow in each length, then trim the ends. Glue a bow to each pocket flap. Turn the calendar over. For hanger loops, cut two 4-inch lengths of gold cord. Fold each length in half to form a loop, and glue the ends of a loop in each of the top corners on the back of the calendar.

glue

Patterns

(top)

small pocket
(cut 6)

FOLD

large flap
(cut 1)

FOLD

small flap
(cut 6)

FOLD

(top)

large pocket
(cut 1)

FOLD

Super Snowman Magnet

WHAT YOU'LL NEED

Tracing paper

Pencil

Scissors

Craft foam:
white, blue,
brown, orange,
black

Craft glue

2 wiggle eyes,
7mm each

Tweezers

3 black buttons,
7/16 inch each

5½-inch strip
adhesive-back
magnet

1 Trace and cut out the patterns on page 61.

Patterns

scarf

hat

nose

arm
(cut 2)

body

2 Using the patterns, trace the shapes on the following colors of foam: snowman body on white, scarf on blue, twig arms on brown (make 2), carrot nose on orange, and hat on black. Cut out the pieces.

3 With the craft glue, attach the hat to the snowman's head, the scarf to the neck, the twig arms on both sides of the snowman's upper body, and the nose to the middle of the face. Use tweezers to help you glue the wiggle eyes above the nose. Glue the buttons down the center of the body.

4 Peel the backing off the magnet strip, and attach the magnet to the back of the snowman.

Contents

Swirling Paper Twirls

WHAT YOU'LL NEED

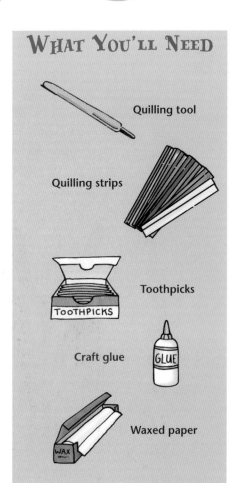

Quilling tool

Quilling strips

Toothpicks

Craft glue

Waxed paper

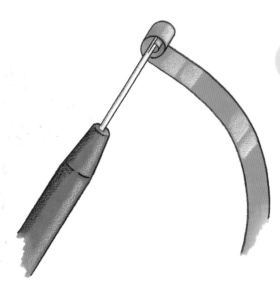

1 To make a circular twirl, slip the end of a quilling strip into the slit on the quilling tool, and gently roll the paper around itself. Let go, and slip the paper twirl off the tool. Use a toothpick to apply a bit of glue to the outside end of the paper strip to create a round shape.

2 Create a variety of shapes by using different lengths of quilling strips and pinching paper twirls. Try these simple shapes in combinations to create your own design:

Teardrop—Repeat step 1 to make a circular twirl, and pinch 1 edge.

Triangle—Repeat step 1 to make a circular twirl, and pinch 3 edges.

Heart—Fold a paper strip in half, and twirl each end toward the middle.

S-shape—Twirl one end of a quilling strip toward the middle. Twirl the other end in the other direction toward the middle.

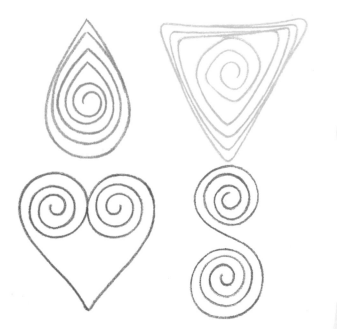

3 Lay the finished shapes on waxed paper. Glue the shapes together to create various designs.

Try This!
Attach your finished designs to blank note cards, or frame them in a shadowbox against a black paper background.

3

Ladybug Pencil Holder

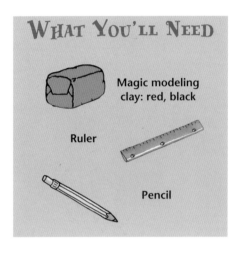

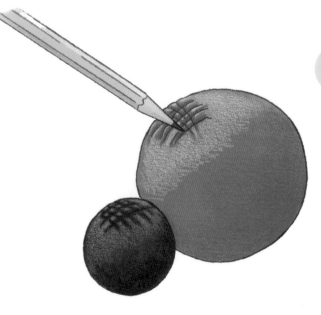

1 From the red clay, make a large ball approximately 5 inches in diameter. From the black clay, make a smaller ball approximately 2 inches in diameter. Scrape a small area of the surface of each ball with a pencil tip to create a textured patch. Gently push the balls together at the textured areas, then gently push the entire shape against your work surface to flatten the bottom of the ladybug.

2 Use the edge of a ruler or plastic knife to make a line down the center of the ladybug's back. Form 6 small ½-inch balls of black clay, and gently flatten them onto the back of the ladybug (see illustration for placement).

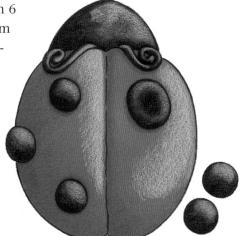

3 Use a pencil tip to create eyes and a mouth. Firmly poke the pencil through the black spots on the ladybug's back. Let dry 24 hours.

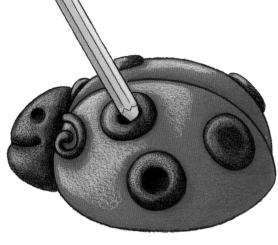

Did You Know?
Many centuries ago farmers prayed to Mary, the mother of Jesus, to stop the swarms of pests that were destroying their crops. Soon after, ladybugs came and ate the bad pests. The farmers called these bugs "Beetles of Our Lady," which eventually became shortened to "ladybugs"!

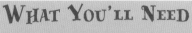

Plastic Canvas Bookmarks

What You'll Need

Red bookmark

Yarn: 60-inch length white, 84-inch length navy blue

2×6-inch piece red plastic canvas

4 red, white, and blue stickers, about 1½ inches each

Pink bookmark

Yarn: 60-inch length dark pink, 84-inch length turquoise

2×6-inch piece light pink plastic canvas

4 pink, purple, and turquoise stickers, about 1½ inches each

Green bookmark

Yarn: 60-inch length white, 84-inch length purple

2×6-inch piece green plastic canvas

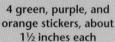

4 green, purple, and orange stickers, about 1½ inches each

All bookmarks

Large-eyed needle

Ruler

Scissors

1 (Use desired color yarn and plastic canvas.) Tie a knot in one end of the 60-inch length of yarn. Knot again. Thread the other end of the yarn through the needle. Beginning in the middle of the small edge of the canvas, insert the needle from the back; pull yarn through to the front. Wrap the yarn around the edge of the canvas and back up through the next square. Continue stitching, placing the needle through the corner squares twice, 1 stitch on each side of the corner. When you've gone around the entire edge of the canvas, tie a double knot in the yarn in the back of the canvas.

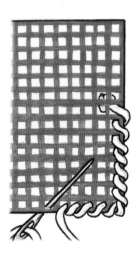

2 To make tassels, cut the 84-inch length of yarn into twelve 7-inch lengths. Thread one 7-inch length onto the needle, and insert it through the third square from the left in the row above the border. Repeat with 2 more lengths in the same hole. Align all yarn ends, and tie a knot. Repeat to make 3 more tassels, leaving 2 empty squares between each tassel.

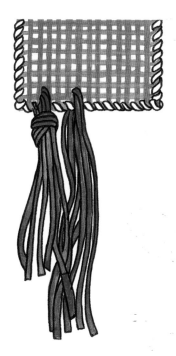

3 Attach 2 stickers to the front of the bookmark and 2 stickers to the back.

Did You Know?
The largest library in the United States is the Library of Congress in Washington, D.C. Its collection includes more than 28 million books. That's a lot of bookmarks!

WHAT YOU'LL NEED

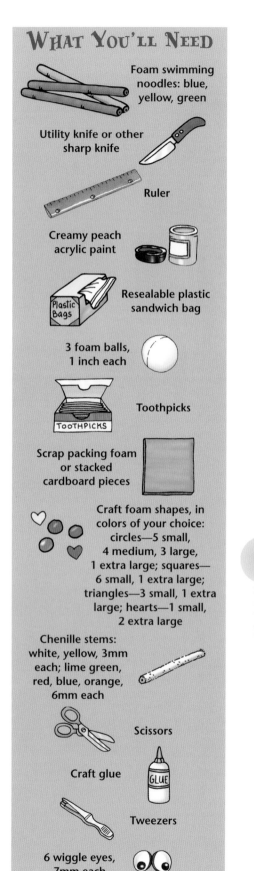

Foam swimming noodles: blue, yellow, green

Utility knife or other sharp knife

Ruler

Creamy peach acrylic paint

Resealable plastic sandwich bag

3 foam balls, 1 inch each

Toothpicks

Scrap packing foam or stacked cardboard pieces

Craft foam shapes, in colors of your choice: circles—5 small, 4 medium, 3 large, 1 extra large; squares— 6 small, 1 extra large; triangles—3 small, 1 extra large; hearts—1 small, 2 extra large

Chenille stems: white, yellow, 3mm each; lime green, red, blue, orange, 6mm each

Scissors

Craft glue

Tweezers

6 wiggle eyes, 7mm each

Nutsy Noodles

Adult help needed

1 Ask an adult to use a utility knife to cut a 1-inch slice from each color of foam swimming noodle. Have him or her cut the yellow slice in half.

2 Pour a small amount of creamy peach acrylic paint into the sandwich bag. Drop the foam balls in the bag, and close the bag. Roll the balls around inside the bag until they are completely coated with paint. Add more paint if needed. Use toothpicks to remove the balls from the bag. With a foam ball pressed onto one end of a toothpick, insert the opposite end into a piece of packing foam or stacked layers of cardboard to dry.

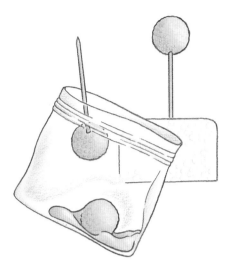

3 To make a funny hat for your Nutsy Noodle boy and girl, poke a hole in a craft foam shape with one end of a chenille stem. Slide the foam shape onto the chenille stem, and repeat to add more shapes. (The boy hat is made with foam squares on a 3mm white chenille stem. The girl hat is made with a 6mm lime green chenille stem, foam circles, and 2 extra-large yellow hearts.) Fold the chenille stem over the top of the hat about ¼ inch to prevent the wire from poking you. Cut the other end ½ inch below the bottom of the hat, add a drop of glue, and insert it into a 1-inch foam ball.

4 To make the head of the Nutsy Noodle puppy, use a toothpick to make a slit on each side of a foam ball. Add a drop of glue on a corner of a small foam triangle, then insert the corner into the slit in the foam ball. Repeat with the other foam triangle. Glue a small heart onto the foam ball for the puppy's muzzle.

5 Cut three 1-inch lengths from tooth-picks. Add a drop of glue on the cut end of each toothpick, then insert them into the bottom of each foam ball. Let dry. Add a drop of glue to the pointed end of each toothpick, then insert them into the noodle slices. Use tweezers to glue 2 wiggle eyes on each foam ball. Glue a small triangle onto an extra large triangle, then glue the extra-large triangle to the front of the Nutsy Noodle boy for his collar. Cut a red and blue chenille stem in half, then fold each half in half. Insert folded pieces into the bottom of the foam noodles for shoes as shown.

6 Wrap the orange chenille stem around the puppy's neck to make a collar. Twist the stem in the back, cut off excess, and fold down the twisted ends. Spiral-wrap a yellow chenille stem around a toothpick, take the toothpick out, and then insert one end of the stem into the foam noodle for the tail. Cut excess.

Try This!
Go nuts, and make an entire neighborhood of Nutsy Noodles with foam shapes and foam swimming noodles. Don't stop with people—use your imagination to make a cat, a bird, or even a scary monster!

10

Doily Angel

WHAT YOU'LL NEED

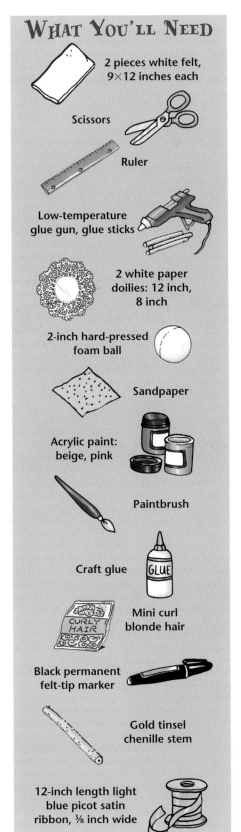

2 pieces white felt, 9×12 inches each

Scissors

Ruler

Low-temperature glue gun, glue sticks

2 white paper doilies: 12 inch, 8 inch

2-inch hard-pressed foam ball

Sandpaper

Acrylic paint: beige, pink

Paintbrush

Craft glue

Mini curl blonde hair

Black permanent felt-tip marker

Gold tinsel chenille stem

12-inch length light blue picot satin ribbon, ⅜ inch wide

Adult help needed

1   Use the pattern on page 13 to cut an angel dress out of white felt. Roll the felt dress into a cone shape, overlapping the straight sides 2 inches on the bottom of the dress and ½ inch at the neckline. Glue the overlapped edges together.

11

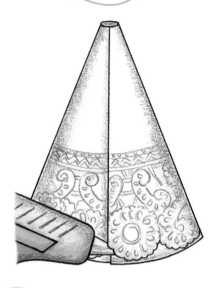

2 Cut the 12-inch doily in half; discard the other half. Trace just the neckline of the dress pattern on the doily. Trim away the doily above the neckline. Wrap the doily around the felt dress, overlapping the straight edges at the back. Glue in place. Use a few drops of glue to attach the doily to the felt dress at the back.

3 Use the pattern on page 13 to cut an angel wing out of white felt. Roll the felt wing into a cone shape, overlapping the straight edges 1 inch at the bottom of the wing and tapering to a point at the top. Glue in place. Cut the 8-inch doily in half; set the other half aside. Wrap the doily around the wing, overlapping the straight edges at the side seam; glue. Use a few drops of glue to attach the doily to the felt wing at the side seam. Apply glue to the side seam of the wing, and place it at the side of the dress. The top point of the wing should be even with the dress neckline. Repeat for the second wing.

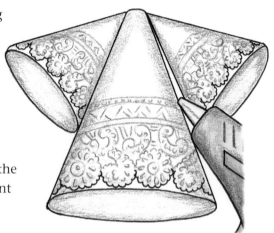

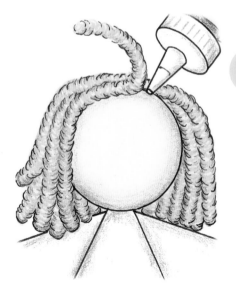

4 To make the angel's head, lightly sand the foam ball. Paint the ball with 2 coats of beige; let dry. Using the glue gun, apply glue to the neckline of the dress and place the head into the glue. For hair, apply craft glue to the top, sides, and back of the head. Gently fluff the mini curl hair, and place it into the glue, slightly overlapping the curls. Spot-glue and add more hair as needed. Paint the angel's cheeks pink; let dry. Use the marker to draw the eyes, eyebrows, nose, and mouth (see illustration on page 11).

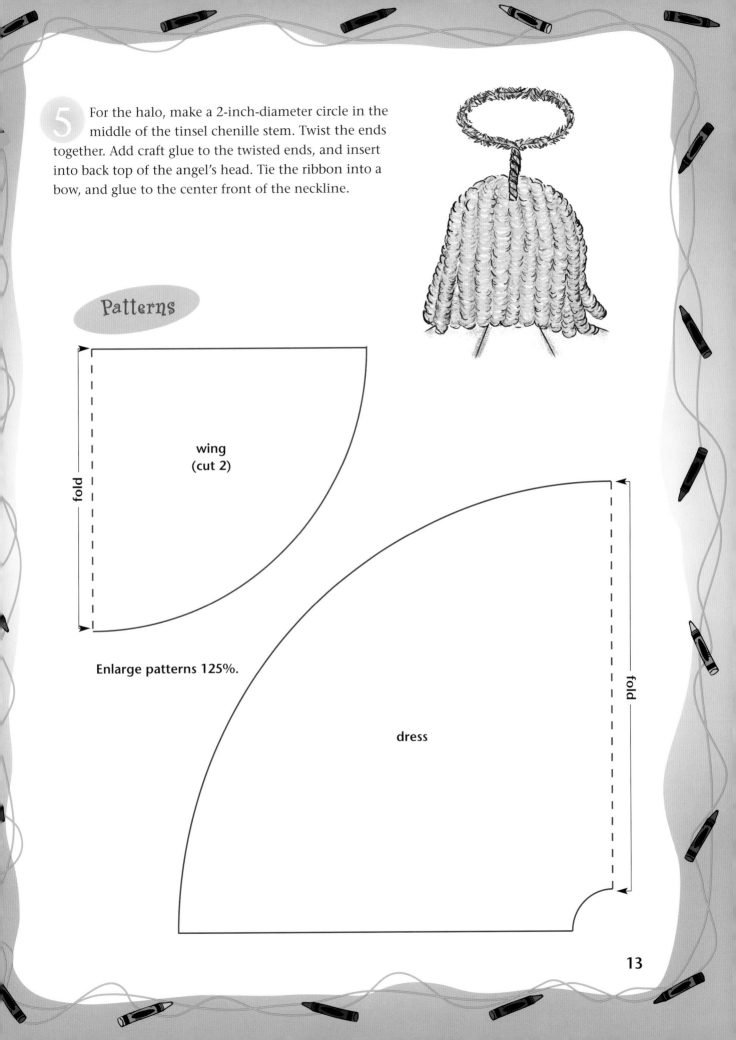

5 For the halo, make a 2-inch-diameter circle in the middle of the tinsel chenille stem. Twist the ends together. Add craft glue to the twisted ends, and insert into back top of the angel's head. Tie the ribbon into a bow, and glue to the center front of the neckline.

Patterns

fold

wing
(cut 2)

Enlarge patterns 125%.

dress

fold

High-Flying Kite

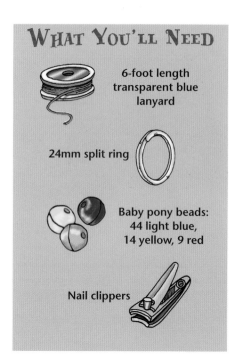

1 Fold the lanyard in half, and slip the looped end through the split ring. Pull the cut ends up through the loop, and pull tight.

Did You Know?
The world record for the longest "kite fly" is 180 hours!

2 String a light blue bead onto the left strand and slide it all the way up. Weave the right strand through the bead from right to left. Now slide 3 light blue beads onto the left strand. Weave the right strand through the beads from right to left.

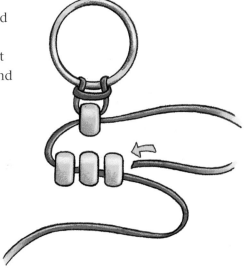

3 Keep stringing and weaving in this manner, following the diagram. Be sure to pull the cords firmly and to keep the lanyard flat as you weave each row.

4 Finish the body of the kite by tying both lanyard ends in an overhand knot. To do this, twist both lanyard ends into a loop and then pull the free ends through the loop. Tie a second overhand knot about ½ inch from the first, then string 1 red bead on each strand of lanyard followed by another overhand knot—this creates the "bows" that weight the tail of the kite. Repeat this process to make 2 more bows with yellow and light blue beads. Use nail clippers to trim the excess lanyard, leaving ½-inch tails.

Dinosaur Magnet

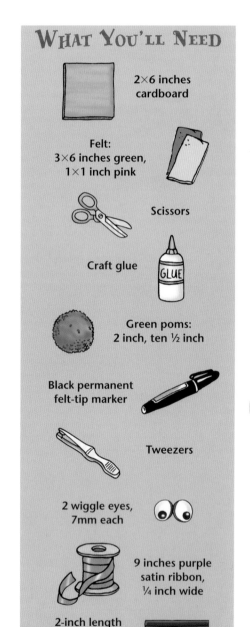
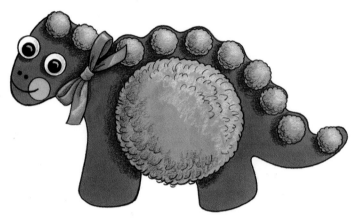

1 Use the body pattern on page 17 to cut a dinosaur out of cardboard and green felt. Cover the cardboard cutout with the felt cutout; glue in place.

16

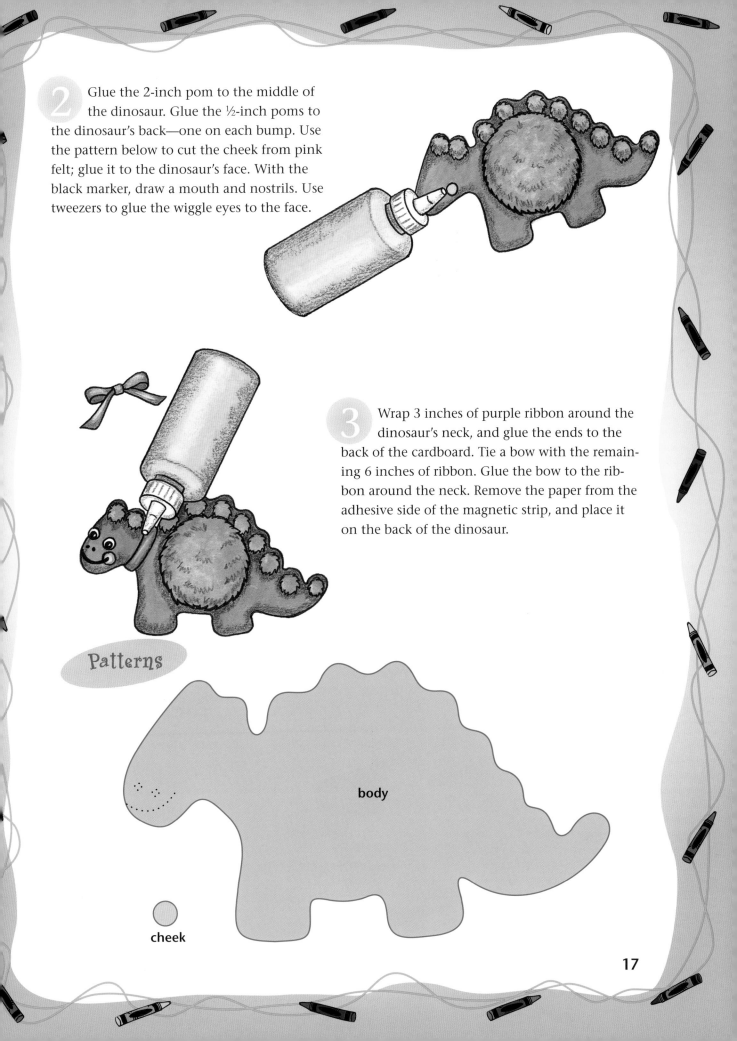

2 Glue the 2-inch pom to the middle of the dinosaur. Glue the ½-inch poms to the dinosaur's back—one on each bump. Use the pattern below to cut the cheek from pink felt; glue it to the dinosaur's face. With the black marker, draw a mouth and nostrils. Use tweezers to glue the wiggle eyes to the face.

3 Wrap 3 inches of purple ribbon around the dinosaur's neck, and glue the ends to the back of the cardboard. Tie a bow with the remaining 6 inches of ribbon. Glue the bow to the ribbon around the neck. Remove the paper from the adhesive side of the magnetic strip, and place it on the back of the dinosaur.

Patterns

body

cheek

Pom-Pom Mirror

Adult help needed

WHAT YOU'LL NEED

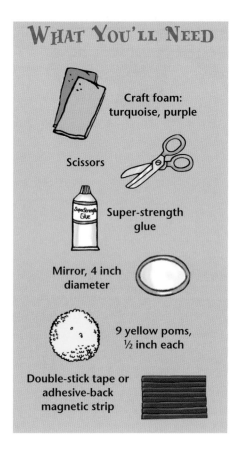

Craft foam: turquoise, purple

Scissors

Super-strength glue

Mirror, 4 inch diameter

9 yellow poms, ½ inch each

Double-stick tape or adhesive-back magnetic strip

1 Use the patterns on page 19 to cut flowers out of turquoise and purple foam.

18

2 Center the purple petals over the turquoise petals, and glue them together. Be sure the area you are working in is well ventilated.

3 Glue the mirror to the center of the purple petals. Glue the poms around the mirror. Use double-stick tape to attach the finished mirror to a surface, or add an adhesive-back magnetic strip to hang the mirror on your locker or other metal surface.

Enlarge patterns 145%.

Patterns

fold

What You'll Need

5×7-inch wood picture frame

8×10-inch piece coarse nylon net

Staple gun, staples

1-gallon bucket

Large brown paper grocery bag

Large slotted spoon

Blender

Deep plastic dishpan

21×21 inches old sheet

20×20 inches flat, smooth, nonporous plastic or similar material

Sponge

Clothesline and clothespins

Adult help needed

1 Take the glass and backing off the picture frame. Ask an adult to help you staple the nylon net across the back of the frame, stretching the net tightly. Set aside. Fill a bucket halfway with warm water. Tear the grocery bag into 2-inch squares. Drop the pieces into the bucket of water, and stir with the slotted spoon. Let soak ½ hour.

2 Add the soaked paper to the blender with an equal amount of water a little at a time. Don't overload the blender, and use plenty of water. Have an adult help you blend the paper on low speed, then medium speed until it becomes pulpy. Don't overblend. Fill the dishpan halfway with warm water. Pour the pulp into the pan.

3 Hold the frame horizontally, net side up. As you lower it into the pan of pulp, tilt it down and scoop under the pulp, moving it away from your body. Tilt it horizontally under the water and lift up, shaking it slightly. Do this in one smooth, continuous motion. If the pulp is too lumpy or has holes, dump it back into the pan and start over.

4 Let the pulp on the frame drain for a moment over the pan. Wet the sheet and smooth it onto the flat plastic, removing any air bubbles. It's important that the sheet be flat and stuck to the surface; if not, the pulp will not come off the netting later. Turn the frame with the pulp upside-down, setting it onto the wet sheet. Use a sponge to press out as much water as possible. Do not rub. When most of the water has been removed, lift the frame away from the pulp. The pulp should stick to the sheet. If it does not stick or if there are holes, dump it back into the pan of pulp and start over.

5 Once the pulp is stuck to the sheet, pin the sheet to the clothesline until the piece of paper on it is dry. Then carefully peel away the paper. Make more pieces and put them together to make a notebook, or use your handmade paper for writing notes. You could also make a fall collage on the paper with real leaves or leaf cutouts.

WHAT YOU'LL NEED

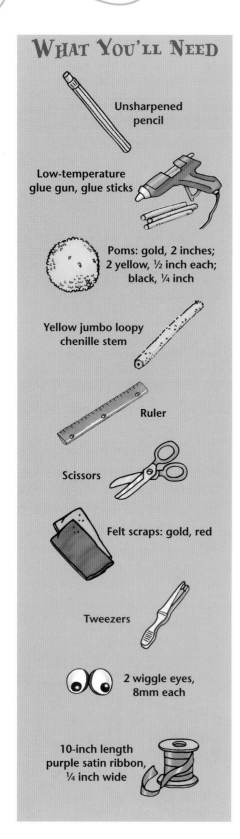

Unsharpened pencil

Low-temperature glue gun, glue sticks

Poms: gold, 2 inches; 2 yellow, ½ inch each; black, ¼ inch

Yellow jumbo loopy chenille stem

Ruler

Scissors

Felt scraps: gold, red

Tweezers

2 wiggle eyes, 8mm each

10-inch length purple satin ribbon, ¼ inch wide

Adult help needed

1 Apply glue to the top and sides of the pencil eraser, and insert it into the gold pom, pushing the sides of the pom into the glue on the sides of the eraser.

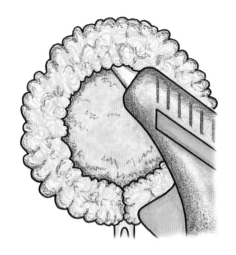

2 The back of the lion will be the printed side of the pencil. Cut a 7-inch length from the chenille stem, and glue one end to the back of the pencil just below the pom. Wrap and curve the chenille stem up and over the top of the pom. Glue the other end to the back of the pencil, just meeting the first end on the back. Spot-glue the chenille stem to the top of the pom.

3 Use the patterns below to cut 2 ears from gold felt and a tongue from red felt. Glue the ears to the pom where the mane and pom meet. For jowls, glue 2 yellow poms to the face just below the center. Glue the tongue below and between the jowls. To make the nose, glue the black pom at the top middle of the jowls. Use tweezers to glue the wiggle eyes to the face so the bottom edges of the eyes touch the top of the jowls. Spot-glue the eyes to the jowls to hold.

4 Wrap the purple satin ribbon around the pencil just below the pom, and tie a bow. Spot-glue the ribbon to the pencil.

Patterns

ear
(cut 2)

tongue

23

Flyaway Plant Pokes

WHAT YOU'LL NEED

Craft foam:
red, blue

Scissors

Low-temperature
glue gun,
glue sticks

Polyester fiberfill

2 wood dowels,
12 inches each

Acrylic paint:
yellow, white

Paintbrush

Black permanent
felt-tip marker

18-inch lengths
plastic-coated wire:
18-gauge blue,
22-gauge red

Wire cutters

Adult help needed

1 Use the patterns on page 25 to cut out 2 cardinal bodies and 2 cardinal wings from red craft foam. Repeat with the bluebird patterns and blue craft foam.

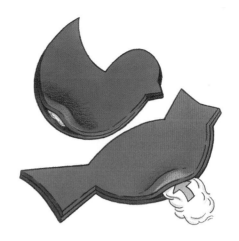

2 Glue the body patterns together, leaving a 1-inch opening in the bottom. Lightly stuff the inside of the foam birds with fiberfill. Poke a dowel inside the opening, and glue closed.

3 Glue the wings to each side of the birds' bodies. Paint the beaks yellow. Use the end of the paintbrush to add white dots on the body and wings of the bluebird. Paint groups of 3 small yellow dots on the body and wings of the cardinal. Draw eyes on both birds with the black marker.

4 Bend the plastic-coated wire around each bird's neck into the shape of a bow. Bend the wire ends so they look nice.

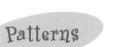

Enlarge patterns 250%.

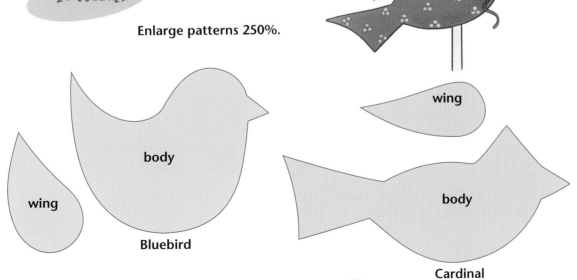

wing

body

wing

body

Bluebird

Cardinal

No-Sew Fleece Purse

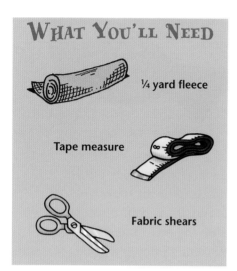

1 Cut a piece of fleece 18×18 inches. Cut a second piece 18×12 inches. Line up the bottoms of the 2 pieces along the 18-inch edges. Make 3-inch slits up from the bottom of both pieces of fabric every ¾ inch. Then make 3-inch slits up both sides every ¾ inch.

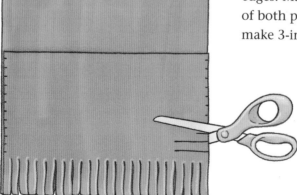

26

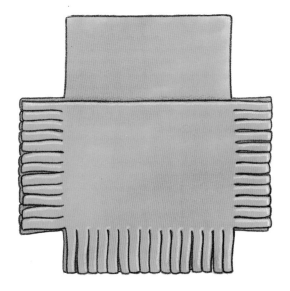

2 Cut out the bottom corners of both pieces. Cut in the sides of the larger piece to make a flap for the purse.

3 Tie each slit, front piece to back piece, in a double knot. Leave the last 2 slits on the top corners of the fabric untied.

4 To make a handle, cut 3 strips of fleece 1×26 inches each. Tie the 3 pieces together at one end, and braid. Tie the ends in a knot. Tie the top slits on each side of the purse around the braids to hold the handle.

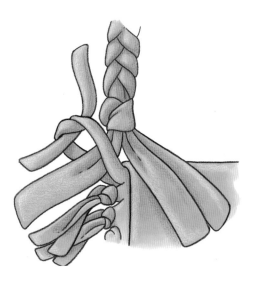

Sly Snake Zipper Pull

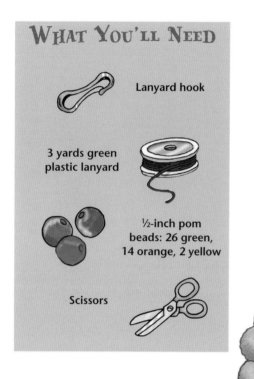

What You'll Need

Lanyard hook

3 yards green plastic lanyard

½-inch pom beads: 26 green, 14 orange, 2 yellow

Scissors

1. Thread the plastic lanyard through the lanyard hook, forming 2 even tails. String a green pom bead on 1 lace. String the other lace through the same bead in the opposite direction. Pull the bead snug to the lanyard hook. String 2 green pom beads on 1 lace. String the other lace through the same beads in the opposite direction. Pull snug against the first pom bead.

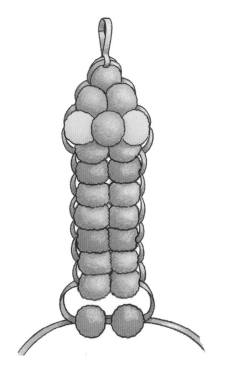

2 String 1 yellow pom bead, 1 green, and another yellow on 1 lace. String the other lace through the same beads in the opposite direction. Pull snug to the second row of pom beads. On the next row, string 2 green pom beads on 1 lace. String the other lace through the same beads in the opposite direction. Repeat, this time with a row of 2 orange pom beads. Continue in this manner with 2 rows of green beads and 1 row of orange beads until you have 18 total rows.

3 To make the tail, string a green pom bead on 1 lace. String the other lace through the same bead in the opposite direction. Pull snug. Add a single orange row, a single green row, and 3 more single orange rows. Tie the laces in a double knot, and trim the ends. Attach this zipper pull to your backpack for a sleek, sly look!

Did You Know?
Contrary to popular belief, snake skin is not clammy or slimy but smooth, dry, and slightly cool to the touch.

My Very Own Message Board

WHAT YOU'LL NEED

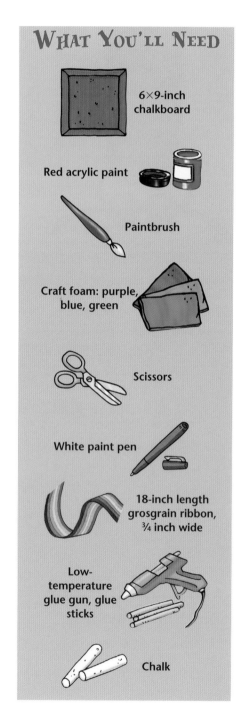

6×9-inch chalkboard

Red acrylic paint

Paintbrush

Craft foam: purple, blue, green

Scissors

White paint pen

18-inch length grosgrain ribbon, ¾ inch wide

Low-temperature glue gun, glue sticks

Chalk

Adult help needed

1   Paint the chalkboard frame red. Let dry, then apply another coat.

2 Use the patterns below to cut the turtle from purple craft foam, the seahorse from blue craft foam, and the alligator from green craft foam. (You may want to use transfer paper to get the pattern details.) Add details on the front of each sea creature with the white paint pen. Let dry.

3 Glue an end of the ribbon to each side of the chalkboard back at the top corners. Position the sea creatures on the front of the chalkboard around the frame; glue in place. Use chalk to write a message on your board, then hang it on your bedroom door to let friends and family know if you are in, out, or just want to be left alone!

Patterns

Enlarge patterns 125%.

Nifty Napkin Holder

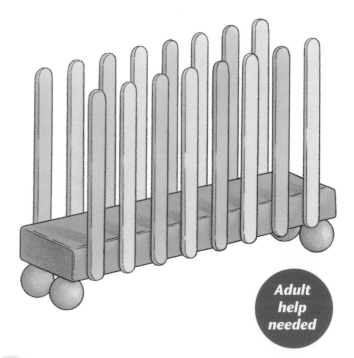

What You'll Need

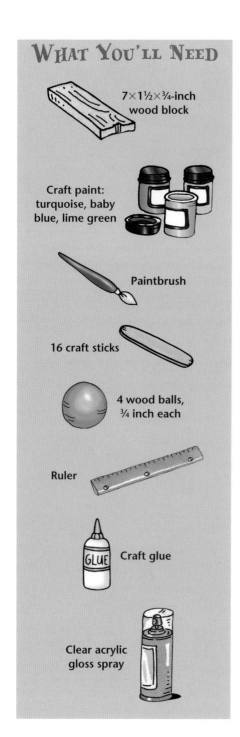

7 × 1½ × ¾-inch wood block

Craft paint: turquoise, baby blue, lime green

Paintbrush

16 craft sticks

4 wood balls, ¾ inch each

Ruler

GLUE Craft glue

Clear acrylic gloss spray

Adult help needed

1 Cover your work surface. Paint the wood block turquoise. Paint both sides of 8 craft sticks baby blue and both sides of the other craft sticks lime green. Paint 4 wood balls lime green. Let all pieces dry for at least 20 minutes.

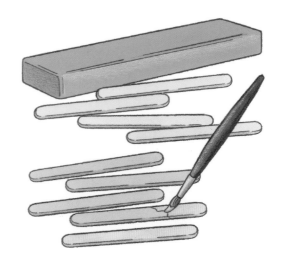

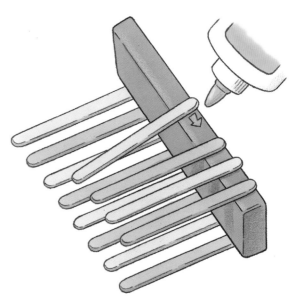

2   Beginning ½ inch in from one end of the base, alternate gluing lime green and baby blue craft sticks ⅜ inches apart along one side. Let dry 20 minutes. Turn the base over, and repeat to glue the remaining 8 sticks to the other side.

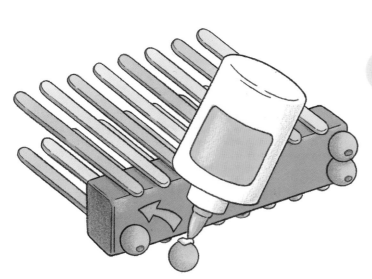

3   Glue a ball to each of the bottom corners of the wood block. Let dry 20 minutes. Ask an adult to apply gloss spray to the napkin holder. (Be sure to work in a well-ventilated area.) Let holder dry for 30 minutes.

Try This!
Change the paint colors you use on the Nifty Napkin Holder for a completely different look. You can also add polka dots and other small details with paint, or use small stickers to decorate the holder.

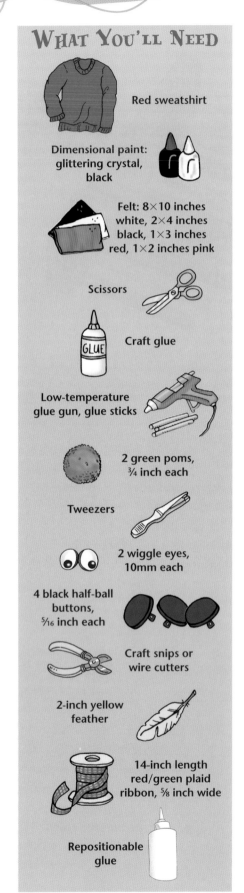

Red sweatshirt

Dimensional paint: glittering crystal, black

Felt: 8×10 inches white, 2×4 inches black, 1×3 inches red, 1×2 inches pink

Scissors

Craft glue

Low-temperature glue gun, glue sticks

2 green poms, ¾ inch each

Tweezers

2 wiggle eyes, 10mm each

4 black half-ball buttons, ⁵⁄₁₆ inch each

Craft snips or wire cutters

2-inch yellow feather

14-inch length red/green plaid ribbon, ⅝ inch wide

Repositionable glue

Snowman Sweatshirt

Adult help needed

1 Make the snowflakes on the front of the sweatshirt. With the glittering crystal dimensional paint, draw a 1-inch horizontal line and 1-inch vertical line to form a cross. Then draw ¾-inch diagonal lines to make an X on top of the cross. Add snowflakes wherever you want on the front of the sweatshirt, but be sure to leave a space for the snowman. Let the paint dry, then repeat on the back of the sweatshirt.

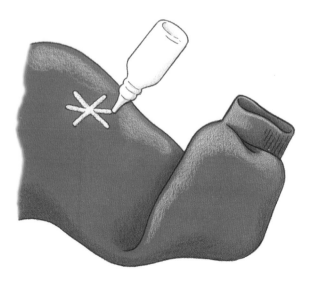

34

2 Use the patterns on page 36 to cut the snowman base, bottom, middle, head, and 2 arms from white felt; hat from black felt; hatband from red felt; and 2 cheeks from pink felt.

3 Use craft glue to attach the parts to the snowman base in the following order: bottom, middle, head, arms, hat, and hatband (see illustration). Use the glue gun to attach a green pom to each side of the head for earmuffs and the cheeks to the face. Use tweezers to glue on wiggle eyes so the bottom edges touch the top of the cheeks. Add a mouth from cheek to cheek with black dimensional paint. Ask an adult to cut the shanks off the buttons with craft snips. Glue 1 button above the mouth for a nose, and glue the remaining buttons down the middle of the snowman. Tuck and glue the end of the feather under the hatband. For the scarf, cut the length of ribbon in half. Then glue the ends of the lengths of ribbon to the back of the snowman's neck. Wrap the ribbons around the front, and knot them.

4 Turn over the snowman, and apply 2 or 3 coats of repositionable glue according to the manufacturer's instructions. Let the glue dry 24 hours, and attach the snowman to the front of the shirt. Be sure to take off the snowman before washing the sweatshirt.

Patterns

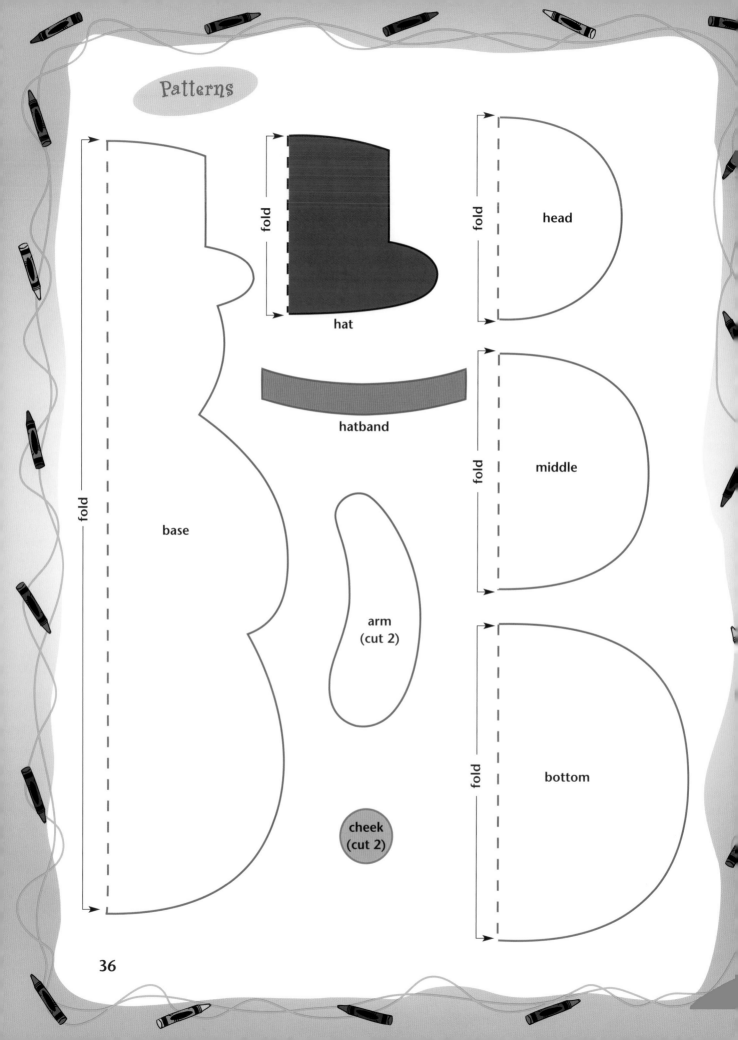

fold

hat

fold

head

fold

base

hatband

fold

middle

arm
(cut 2)

fold

bottom

cheek
(cut 2)

WHAT YOU'LL NEED

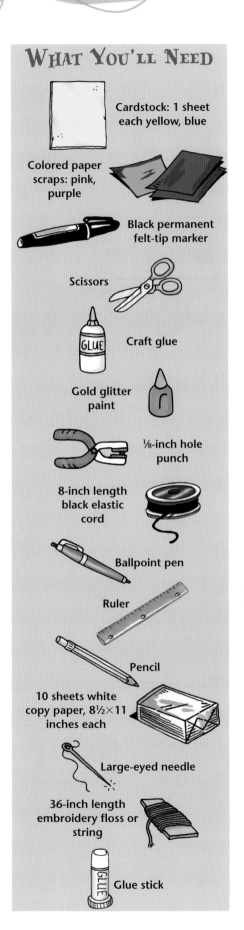

Cardstock: 1 sheet each yellow, blue

Colored paper scraps: pink, purple

Black permanent felt-tip marker

Scissors

Craft glue

Gold glitter paint

⅛-inch hole punch

8-inch length black elastic cord

Ballpoint pen

Ruler

Pencil

10 sheets white copy paper, 8½×11 inches each

Large-eyed needle

36-inch length embroidery floss or string

Glue stick

1 Use the pattern on page 39 to trace the butterfly body on the sheet of yellow cardstock. Trace the wing details on the colored paper. Outline all the pieces with the black felt marker, and cut out.

37

2 Glue the colored details on the wings. Add dots of gold glitter paint to the wings. Let dry. Fold the wings up on the dotted lines. Punch holes where shown on the pattern.

3 Cut the elastic cord in half. Thread one length of cord through each set of holes with the loop on top. Slip the ballpoint pen under the loops. Turn the butterfly over, and tie the elastic ends in a knot on the back. Set the butterfly aside.

4 Cut the blue sheet of cardstock into two 5½-inch squares for the book cover. Measure ½ inch in from an edge of 1 of the squares, and draw a line. Beginning ½ inch in from an edge, mark 5 holes 1⅛ inches apart along this line. Punch a hole on each mark. Repeat for the second square.

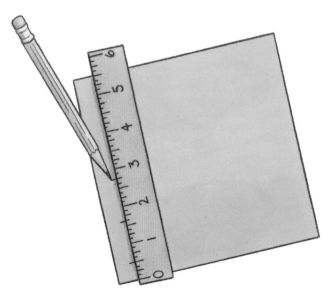

5 Fold each piece of copy paper in half widthwise. Trim excess paper along one side so the pieces measure 5½ inches wide. Use one of the cover squares to mark holes on the folded edge of each piece of paper. Punch holes.

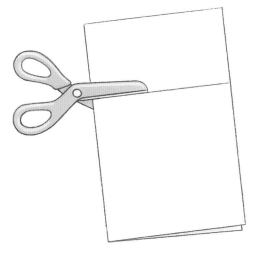

6 Stack the white pages between the book covers, lining up the holes. Thread the needle with floss. Stitch all of the pages and covers together using a running stitch. Start by pushing the needle up through the first hole, leaving a 1½-inch tail of floss in the back. Pull the floss down through the second hole, up through the third, down through the fourth, and up through the fifth. Return the row of running stitches in the opposite direction. Remove the needle, and tie the ends of the floss together at the back of the book. Trim any excess floss. Glue the butterfly to the top of the book along the middle body section, leaving the wings free to flutter!

Pattern

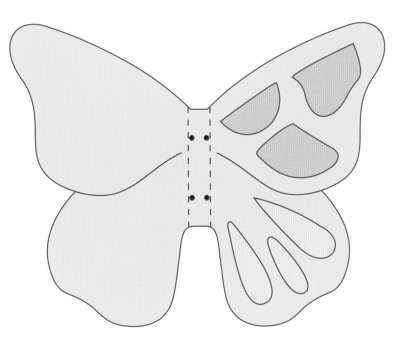

Enlarge patterns 166%.

WHAT YOU'LL NEED

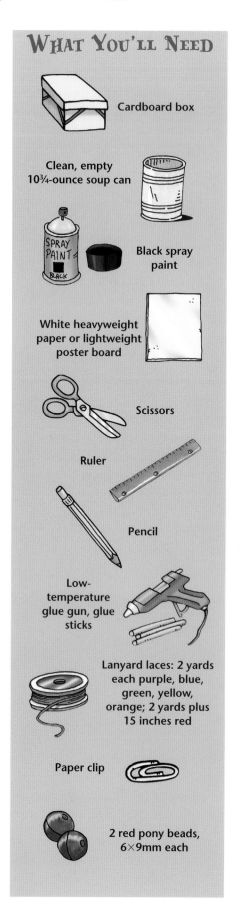

Cardboard box

Clean, empty 10¾-ounce soup can

Black spray paint

White heavyweight paper or lightweight poster board

Scissors

Ruler

Pencil

Low-temperature glue gun, glue sticks

Lanyard laces: 2 yards each purple, blue, green, yellow, orange; 2 yards plus 15 inches red

Paper clip

2 red pony beads, 6×9mm each

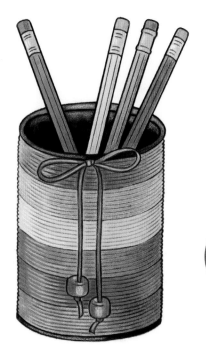

Adult help needed

1 Place the cardboard box on a covered work surface, and put the soup can inside the box. (You may want to complete this step outside or in the garage.) With an adult's help, spray paint the inside, bottom, and rims of the can with black spray paint. Let dry.

2 Cut the paper or poster board to fit around the can. Measure six ⅝-inch horizontal sections on the paper, and draw lines with the pencil to divide the sections. Glue the paper around the can with the lines on the outside.

3 Angle and glue the end of the purple lanyard along the bottom of the can. Begin wrapping the purple lace tightly around the can, covering the glued lace end. Keep the lace flat as you work. Tightly wrap the can 7 or 8 times until you reach the first ⅝-inch mark. At the back of the can, cut any excess lace and glue the lace end to the can.

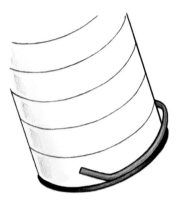

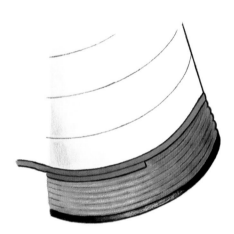

4 To start the next color, glue one end of the blue lace next to the purple lace end. Tightly wrap the blue lace around the can 7 or 8 times to the next ⅝-inch mark. Cut and glue the lace end to the back of the can. Repeat to wrap the can with the green, yellow, orange, and red lanyard laces. Before you finish wrapping the red lanyard, straighten out the end of the paper clip, and place it at the top of the can. Wrap the last 3 red lace rows over the paper clip.

5 Insert the end of the red lanyard through the last 3 wraps, remove the paper clip, and pull the lace tight. Glue the end in place, and trim any excess lanyard. Tie the 15-inch length of red lanyard into a bow. Thread a red pony bead on each lace end, and tie a knot under each bead. Glue the bow to the front of the can.

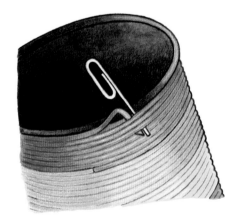

Puddle-Jumping Frog

WHAT YOU'LL NEED

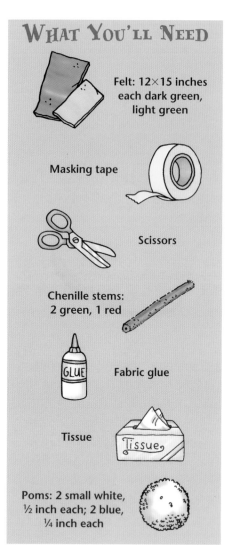

Felt: 12×15 inches each dark green, light green

Masking tape

Scissors

Chenille stems: 2 green, 1 red

Fabric glue

Tissue

Poms: 2 small white, ½ inch each; 2 blue, ¼ inch each

1 Fold dark green felt in half. Lay the frog body pattern from page 44 on the fold, and tape in place. Trace and then cut around the outside of the pattern, making sure not to cut along the fold. Remove tape.

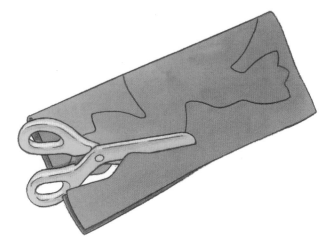

2 Twist a small loop at each end of the green chenille stems. Open the frog, and place 1 chenille stem loop on one of the frog hands. Bend the chenille stem to follow across the arms and mouth, then place the other chenille stem loop on the other frog hand. Glue in place, and hold for 30 seconds. Repeat with the feet, bending the chenille stem to follow the line across the frog's lower body and legs.

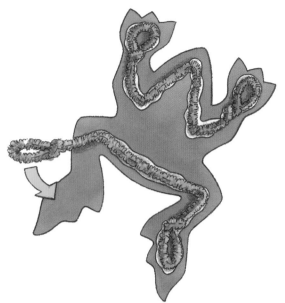

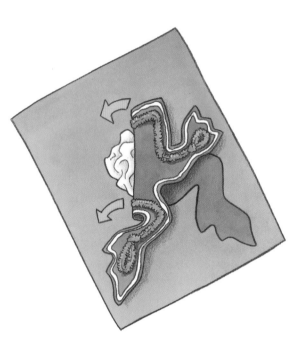

3 Outline the frog with fabric glue. Ball up a few tissues, and place them on the dark felt near the frog's belly. Glue the dark green piece to the light green felt. Cut the red chenille stem in half, and slide it between the frog's mouth before the glue has dried. Press all edges together firmly, and hold for 1 minute. Let dry for 5 minutes.

4 Trim the light green felt around the dark green felt frog. Glue light green felt scraps on the frog's back to create spots. Glue the white poms in place for eyes, and glue on the blue poms for pupils. Curl the tongue. Let dry completely, at least 15 minutes, before posing.

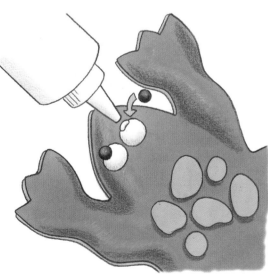

43

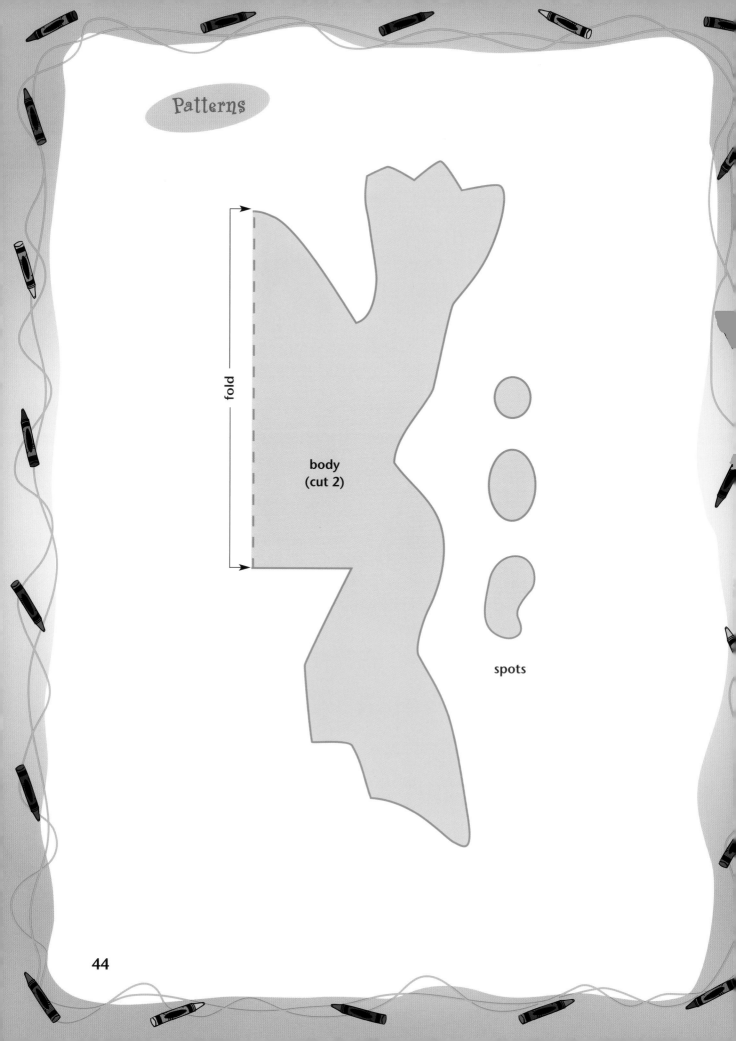

Patterns

fold

body
(cut 2)

spots

44

Hip-Hip Hooray Cheerleader

Adult help needed

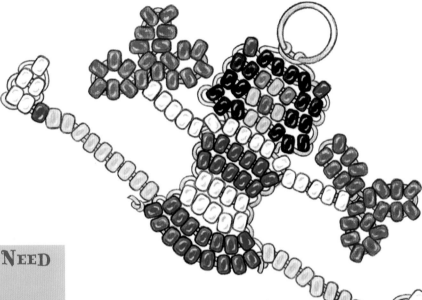

WHAT YOU'LL NEED

7-foot length clear plastic lanyard

24mm split ring

Baby pony beads: 18 black, 31 dark blue, 43 red, 35 white, 23 peach, 2 light blue

Nail clippers

Did You Know?

Today, 97 percent of all high school cheerleaders are female. But back when cheerleading began—more than 100 years ago—all cheerleaders were male. Boy, how times change!

1 Fold the lanyard in half, and slip the looped end through the split ring. Pull the cut ends up through the loop and pull tight. Begin at the top of the cheerleader's head by stringing 4 black baby pony beads onto the left strand. Weave the right strand through the beads from right to left. Add 1 dark blue baby pony bead to each strand. Follow the diagram on the right to string and weave the next 2 rows of beads, counting the beads carefully as the colors change to create the cheerleader's face and hair. Be sure to pull the cords firmly and to keep the lanyard flat as you weave each row. When you get to the fourth row, string beads onto the left strand according to the diagram, and weave the right strand back through all the beads. Now weave the left strand through the second black bead from the left and the right strand through the second black bead from the right.

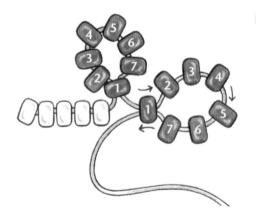

2 For the fifth row, or the cheerleader's arms, start by stringing and weaving 4 white baby pony beads. Add 6 white pony beads to the right strand, then make 3 "sidepaths" with red beads for the cheerleader's pom-poms. To make a sidepath, string on beads 1–7. Leave a little space between the beads, and weave back through bead 1. Pull tightly as you weave back, allowing the beads to curve as shown. Repeat for other 2 sidepaths, then weave the strand back through the last 5 white beads. Repeat for the left arm and pom-pom with the left strand.

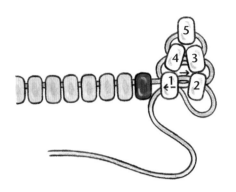

3 Continue weaving and stringing rows 6–10 according to the diagram at the bottom of this page. When you get to row 11, or the legs, string 9 dark blue baby pony beads onto the left strand; weave the right strand back through the beads. Now string 9 peach beads and 1 dark blue bead on the right strand. Make a foot by stringing on beads 1–5. Leave a little space between the beads, and weave back through beads 3, 4 and 1, 2 (allow the beads to curve as shown). Weave back through bead 1 again, then weave the strand through the last dark blue pony bead and 9 peach beads. Repeat for the other leg and foot.

4 Finish by twisting each lanyard end into a loop, and then pull the free end through the loop. Trim any excess lanyard with the nail clippers.

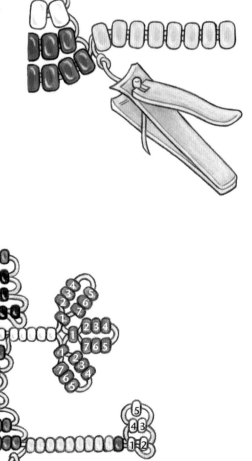

Seed Heart Decoration

WHAT YOU'LL NEED

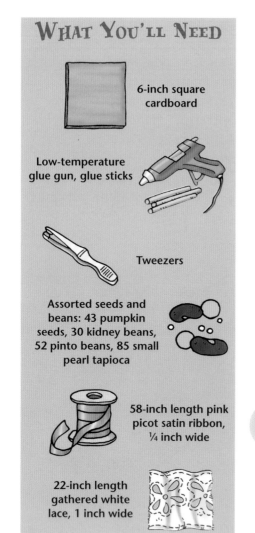

6-inch square cardboard

Low-temperature glue gun, glue sticks

Tweezers

Assorted seeds and beans: 43 pumpkin seeds, 30 kidney beans, 52 pinto beans, 85 small pearl tapioca

58-inch length pink picot satin ribbon, ¼ inch wide

22-inch length gathered white lace, 1 inch wide

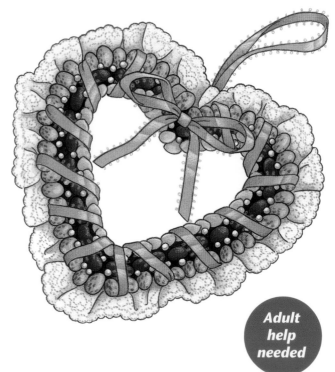

Adult help needed

1 Use the pattern on page 49 to cut a heart out of cardboard. Apply 1 inch of glue to the inside bottom of the heart, and use tweezers to place the pumpkin seeds into the glue, neatly in a row, with each seed slightly overlapping the last. Continue around the inside of heart, applying glue 1 inch at a time until you reach the bottom of the heart again.

2 Repeat the gluing with 2 or 3 more rows of the other seeds (kidney and pinto beans). Fill in spaces with pearl tapioca.

3 Cut two 18-inch lengths and one 12-inch length from the pink picot satin ribbon. Glue one end of an 18-inch length to the top back of the heart, and wrap the ribbon around the heart, through the inside and around the outside until you reach the bottom. Spot-glue the end to the back. Repeat with the other 18-inch length for the other half of the heart. Tie a bow in the 12-inch length of pink ribbon, and glue it to the top middle of the heart.

4 Starting along the back top edge of the heart, apply a few inches of glue and place the binding edge of the 22-inch length of white lace, slightly gathering the lace around the curves.

5 To make a hanger loop, glue together the ends of the remaining 10-inch length of pink ribbon. Glue the ends to the back top of the heart.

Pattern

Enlarge pattern 125%.

fold

Note
Because the seed sizes vary, you may need more or fewer seeds than what is listed on page 48.

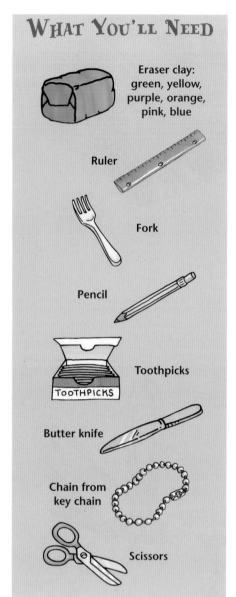

Eraser clay:
green, yellow,
purple, orange,
pink, blue

Ruler

Fork

Pencil

Toothpicks

TOOTHPICKS

Butter knife

Chain from
key chain

Scissors

Cool Clay Key Chain Erasers

Crazy Caterpillar

1 Roll five ½-inch balls and one ¼-inch ball of green clay. Lay them next to each other on a flat surface, with the ¼-inch ball at one end. Gently flatten each ball to about ¼ inch thick so they stick together to form the caterpillar's body. Roll a thin 2-inch length of yellow clay, and lay it along the bottom edge of the body. Use the prongs of a fork to make indents along the yellow clay, sealing it to the body and creating feet.

2 Roll a thin 2-inch length of purple clay, fold it in half, and attach it to the back of the caterpillar's head as antennae, slightly curling the ends. To make the caterpillar's eyes, roll two ⅛-inch balls of yellow clay. Place them on the face, and use a pencil to make an indent in the center of the yellow balls, connecting them to the head. Use a toothpick to make a mouth in the clay.

Majestic Lion

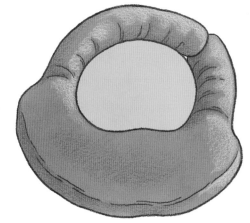

1. Roll a ¾-inch ball of yellow clay. Gently flatten it to about ¼ inch thick to form the lion's face. Roll a tube of orange clay about 5 inches long and ½ inch thick, and lay it around the face. Press the orange clay flat, attaching it to the yellow center.

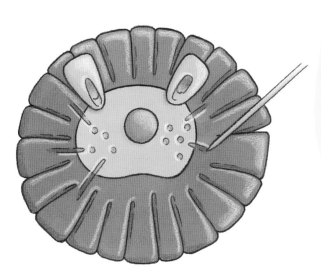

2. Use a butter knife to make lines around the outside to form the mane. Make two ½-inch-long teardrop shapes of yellow clay, and place them on the mane for the lion's ears. Flatten the ears, and indent the middle of them with the fork. For the nose, roll a ¼-inch ball of pink clay and flatten it in the center of the lion's face. Use a toothpick to make freckles and whisker lines. Roll 4 narrow ½-inch lengths of blue clay, and place them on the face for the eyes and mouth. Flatten each length to attach to the yellow face.

Kooky Clown

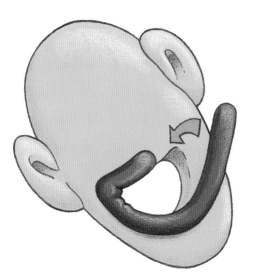

1. Roll an oval about 1½ inches long of yellow clay. Gently flatten it to about ¼ inch thick to form the clown's face. Roll two ¼-inch balls of yellow clay, and flatten them in place as ears on each side of the face. Use a pencil to make an indent in each ear. For the clown's mouth, use a butter knife to make a half circle cutout about ¾ inch wide and ½ inch long. Smooth the edges of the cut clay. Roll a 3-inch length of purple clay, about ¼ inch wide, and lay it around the outer edge of the mouth. Flatten in place to attach.

2 To make the nose, roll a ½-inch ball of pink clay, place it on the face, and flatten it to attach. For eyes, roll two ¼-inch balls of blue clay, put in place, and flatten. Then roll two ⅛-inch balls of yellow clay, put in place on top of the blue clay, and flatten. Use a pencil to poke an indent through both eyes. Add hair by rolling a 1½-inch tube of green clay about ½ inch thick. Flatten the hair to ¼ inch thick, and use a pair of scissors to snip cuts on one edge of the hair. Wrap the unsnipped edge of hair around the top of the head; press in place to attach.

All Key Chains

1 Using the pencil, make a hole in your clay creations where you want to attach the chains. Follow the manufacturer's instructions for baking the clay. Insert the chains through the holes.

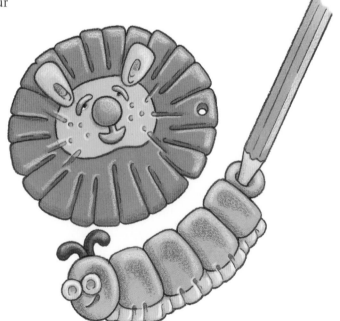

> **Try This!**
> Don't stop now—make all kinds of cool things out of eraser clay and pass them out to your friends and family!

52

WHAT YOU'LL NEED

Wood cutouts:
6 small hearts,
2 medium squares,
4 small triangles

Ruler

Pencil

4 mini craft
sticks, 2½ inches
each

Scissors

3 craft picks

Nail file

Scrap Contac
paper

Masking tape

Permanent markers:
peach, green, yellow,
red, dark blue, light blue

Black permanent
fine-tip marker

Craft glue

4 wiggle eyes,
5mm each

Tweezers

Fishing line,
10 pound test

2 white poms,
5mm

Doggone Purr-fect Cupcake Pokes

HAPPY BIRTHDAY!

AARON

1 To make the puppy's paws, break off the pointed ends of 2 heart wood cutouts. Measure and mark 1½ inches on 2 mini craft sticks. Cut at the marks to make the pets' bodies. Cut off the rounded tip from a craft pick to use as the puppy's tongue. Lightly sand any rough edges with a nail file.

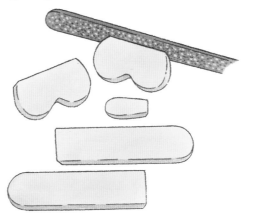

53

2 Peel off the backing from the Contac paper. Tape it to your work surface with the sticky side up. Use markers to color the edges of all the wood pieces. Place the pieces on the Contac paper to hold them in place. Color the front sides of the pieces. Let dry, then turn the pieces over and color the back sides. Do not add color to the bottom 1 to 1½ inches of the craft picks. This part will be inserted into the cupcake.

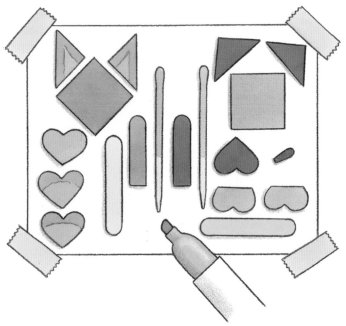

3 Use the fine-tip marker to draw squiggly lines around the outside edges of the pets' bodies, paws, and head pieces to resemble fur. Write "Happy Birthday!" on the uncolored mini craft stick with the fine-tip marker. Then glue the 2 cat paws to the back of the ends of the stick. For the yellow mini craft stick, first glue the puppy's paws at the ends. Then write the birthday boy's or girl's name in the center of the craft stick so it fits between the paws.

4 Glue the head pieces together (see illustration). Let dry, then glue the head to the top of the craft picks. Glue the cut mini craft sticks to the back of the craft pick for the bodies; attach the happy birthday or name sign to the front.

5 Finish the faces by gluing on wiggle eyes using the tweezers. Use the fine-tip black marker to draw the cat's mouth, hair between the puppy's ears, and eyebrows and whisker dots on both pets. Cut four 6-inch lengths of fishing line, and knot them together at the center. Pull tight, then trim the ends to make whiskers. Glue the whiskers with a 5mm pom on the cat's face. Glue the remaining 5mm pom on the puppy's face for a nose.

Try This!
Create a cupcake accent for everyone coming to the birthday party as a party favor. They work great as puppets after the celebration, too!

Milk Bottle Snowman

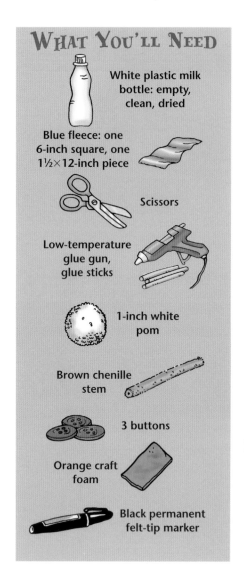

What You'll Need

White plastic milk bottle: empty, clean, dried

Blue fleece: one 6-inch square, one 1½×12-inch piece

Scissors

Low-temperature glue gun, glue sticks

1-inch white pom

Brown chenille stem

3 buttons

Orange craft foam

Black permanent felt-tip marker

Adult help needed

1 Remove the cap from the bottle. Glue the bottom edge of the 6-inch square of fleece around the edge of the bottle cap to create a hat; cut off any excess fleece. Glue the back of the hat closed. Bend down the top of the hat, glue it off to the side, and add the pom.

2 Cut the chenille stem in half. Cut 2 inches off each half, and wrap each 2-inch length around an end of each chenille stem to make hands. Bend the arms, and glue to the sides of the bottle.

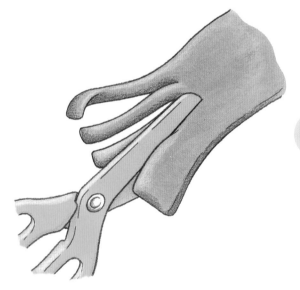

3 For the scarf, cut fringe into the ends of the 1½×12-inch piece of blue fleece. Wrap the scarf around the snowman's neck, and glue it in place. Glue the 3 buttons down the center of the snowman's body. Make a triangle nose out of orange foam; glue it in place. Draw eyes and a mouth with the permanent marker. Fill your snowman with treats, and replace the bottle cap.

> **Note**
> Bottles that are not thoroughly cleaned can become sour. Dishwasher cycles can warp and melt plastic bottles. Use a bottle brush to scrub bottles with soap and hot water.

Fancy Eye Mask

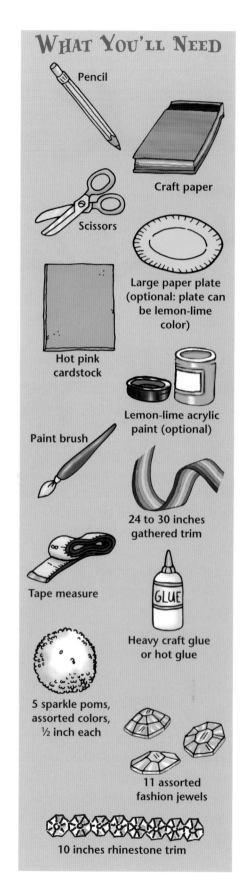

Pencil

Craft paper

Scissors

Large paper plate (optional: plate can be lemon-lime color)

Hot pink cardstock

Lemon-lime acrylic paint (optional)

Paint brush

24 to 30 inches gathered trim

Tape measure

Heavy craft glue or hot glue

5 sparkle poms, assorted colors, ½ inch each

11 assorted fashion jewels

10 inches rhinestone trim

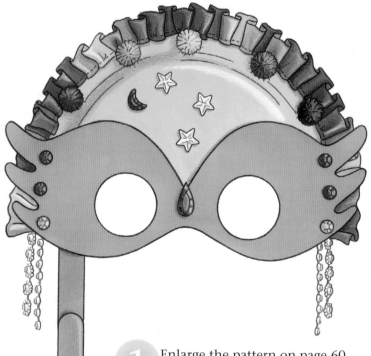

1 Enlarge the pattern on page 60, trace it onto a piece of craft paper, and cut it out. Trace the lower edge of the pattern and the eye holes onto the center of the plate, and cut them out. Trace the pattern onto the cardstock, and cut it out.

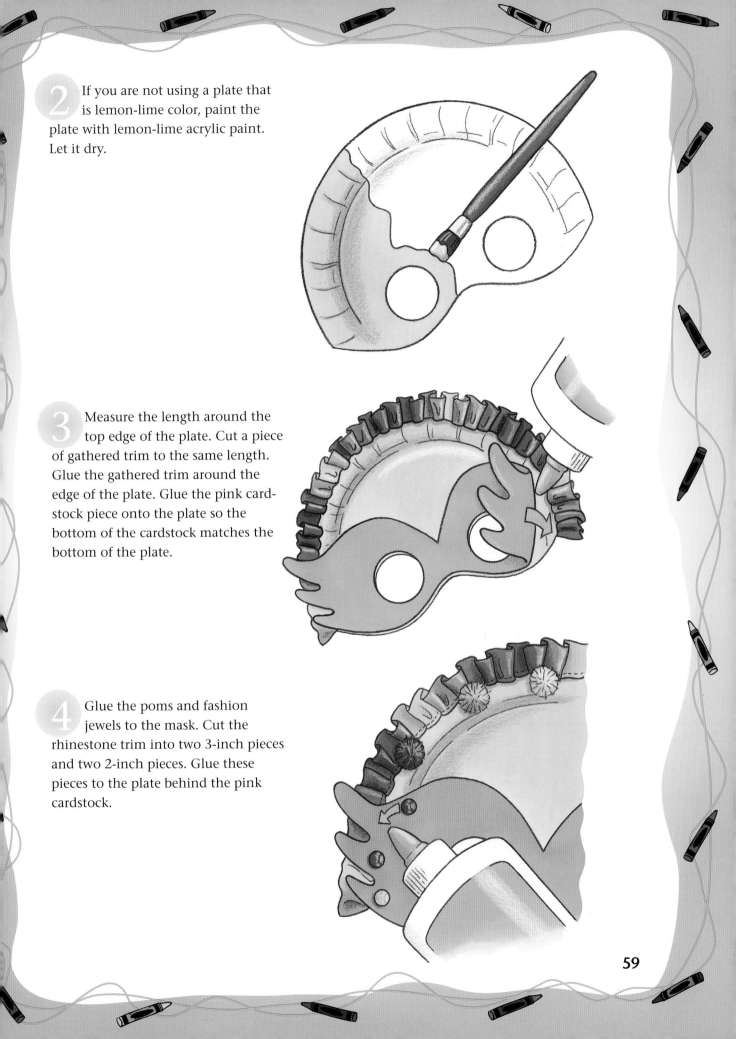

2 If you are not using a plate that is lemon-lime color, paint the plate with lemon-lime acrylic paint. Let it dry.

3 Measure the length around the top edge of the plate. Cut a piece of gathered trim to the same length. Glue the gathered trim around the edge of the plate. Glue the pink card-stock piece onto the plate so the bottom of the cardstock matches the bottom of the plate.

4 Glue the poms and fashion jewels to the mask. Cut the rhinestone trim into two 3-inch pieces and two 2-inch pieces. Glue these pieces to the plate behind the pink cardstock.

5 Put a craft stick on top of another, and glue the ends of one side together. Slide the other stick between first two, overlapping by 2 inches, and glue all the layers together. When the glue is dry, glue the single end of the stick to the back of the plate on the right side.

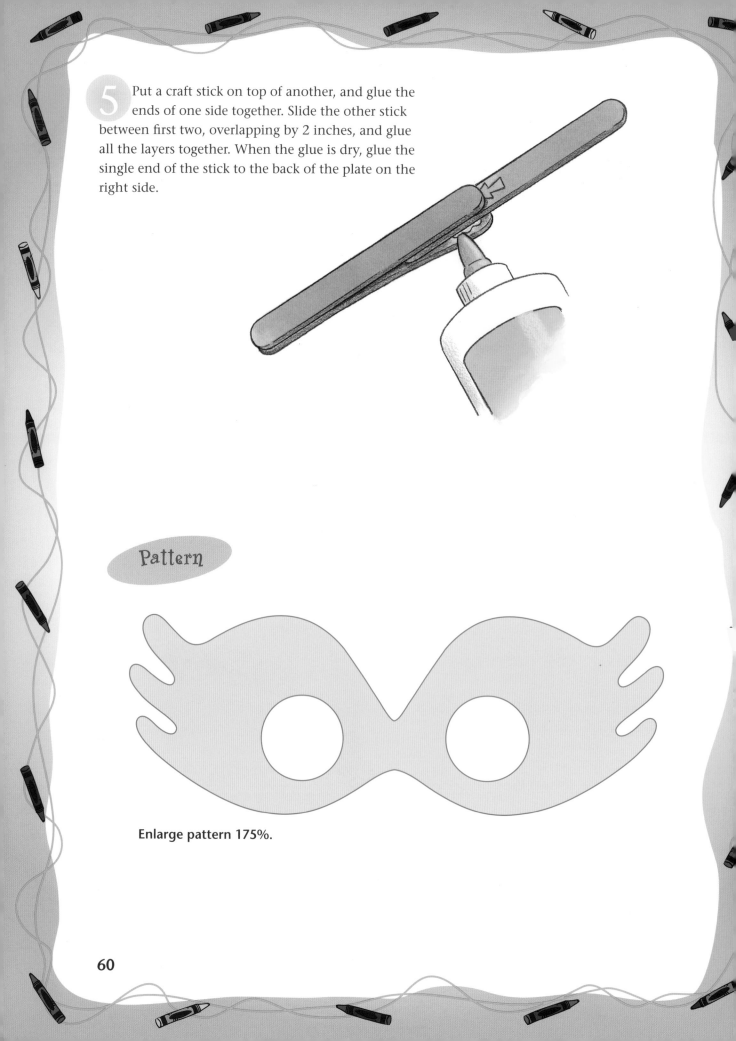

Pattern

Enlarge pattern 175%.

Contents

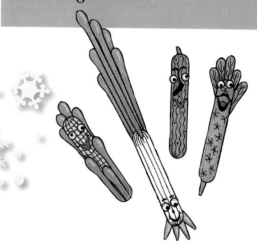

Springtime Fun Finger Puppets

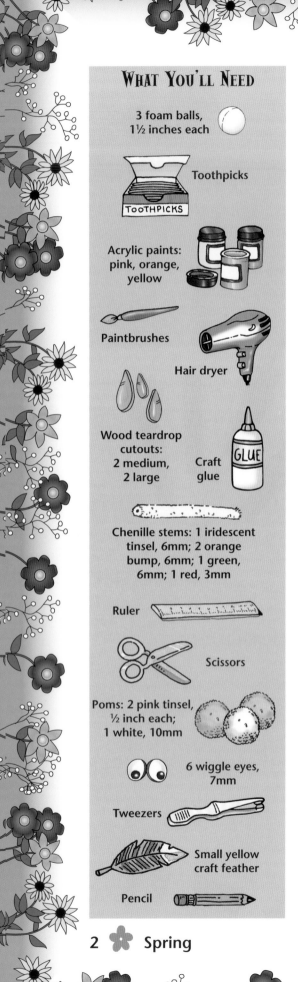

What You'll Need

3 foam balls, 1½ inches each

Toothpicks

Acrylic paints: pink, orange, yellow

Paintbrushes

Hair dryer

Wood teardrop cutouts: 2 medium, 2 large

Craft glue

Chenille stems: 1 iridescent tinsel, 6mm; 2 orange bump, 6mm; 1 green, 6mm; 1 red, 3mm

Ruler

Scissors

Poms: 2 pink tinsel, ½ inch each; 1 white, 10mm

6 wiggle eyes, 7mm

Tweezers

Small yellow craft feather

Pencil

1. Insert a toothpick into each foam ball to help you handle the balls while you decorate them. Paint each ball a different color. Dry the balls with a hair dryer set on a warm temperature, turning them around to dry all sides. Paint 2 medium wood teardrops orange for the duckbill and 2 large teardrops pink for the bunny ears. Dry the wood cutouts with a hair dryer.

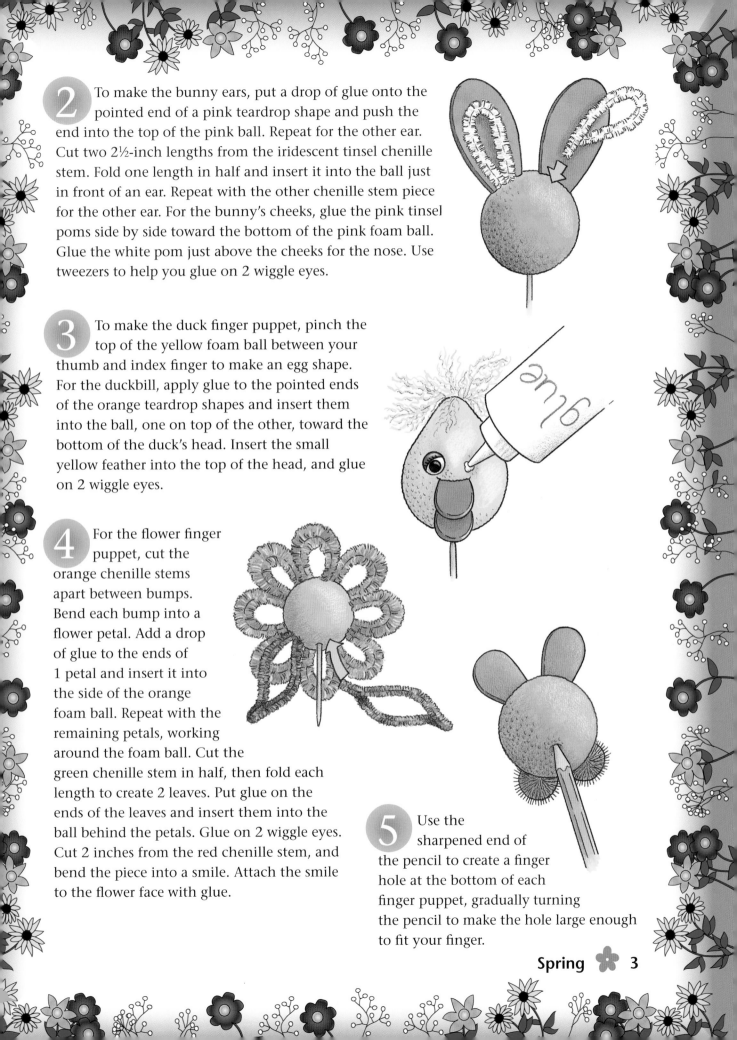

2 To make the bunny ears, put a drop of glue onto the pointed end of a pink teardrop shape and push the end into the top of the pink ball. Repeat for the other ear. Cut two 2½-inch lengths from the iridescent tinsel chenille stem. Fold one length in half and insert it into the ball just in front of an ear. Repeat with the other chenille stem piece for the other ear. For the bunny's cheeks, glue the pink tinsel poms side by side toward the bottom of the pink foam ball. Glue the white pom just above the cheeks for the nose. Use tweezers to help you glue on 2 wiggle eyes.

3 To make the duck finger puppet, pinch the top of the yellow foam ball between your thumb and index finger to make an egg shape. For the duckbill, apply glue to the pointed ends of the orange teardrop shapes and insert them into the ball, one on top of the other, toward the bottom of the duck's head. Insert the small yellow feather into the top of the head, and glue on 2 wiggle eyes.

4 For the flower finger puppet, cut the orange chenille stems apart between bumps. Bend each bump into a flower petal. Add a drop of glue to the ends of 1 petal and insert it into the side of the orange foam ball. Repeat with the remaining petals, working around the foam ball. Cut the green chenille stem in half, then fold each length to create 2 leaves. Put glue on the ends of the leaves and insert them into the ball behind the petals. Glue on 2 wiggle eyes. Cut 2 inches from the red chenille stem, and bend the piece into a smile. Attach the smile to the flower face with glue.

5 Use the sharpened end of the pencil to create a finger hole at the bottom of each finger puppet, gradually turning the pencil to make the hole large enough to fit your finger.

Spring ✿ 3

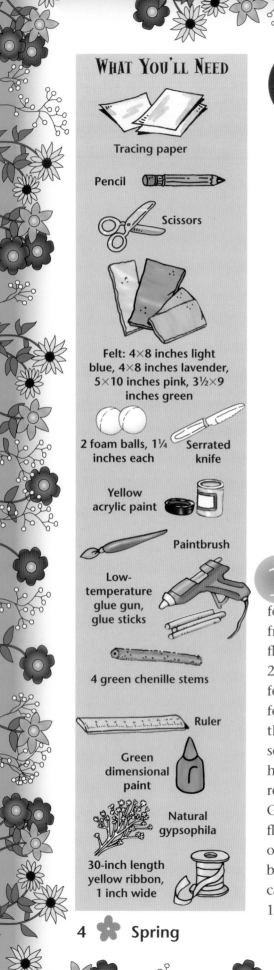

WHAT YOU'LL NEED

Tracing paper

Pencil

Scissors

Felt: 4×8 inches light blue, 4×8 inches lavender, 5×10 inches pink, 3½×9 inches green

2 foam balls, 1¼ inches each

Serrated knife

Yellow acrylic paint

Paintbrush

Low-temperature glue gun, glue sticks

4 green chenille stems

Ruler

Green dimensional paint

Natural gypsophila

30-inch length yellow ribbon, 1 inch wide

Petal Posies

Adult help needed

1 Use the patterns on page 6 to trace and cut out the following: 2 round flowers from light blue felt, 2 round flowers from lavender felt, 2 pointed flowers from pink felt, and 6 leaves from green felt. Have an adult help you cut the foam balls in half with the serrated knife. Paint 3 foam ball halves with yellow paint; discard the remaining ball half. Let paint dry, then apply another coat. Glue the flat side of a ball half to the center of 1 blue flower. To give the flower a dimensional look, apply a line of glue around the very bottom edge of the foam ball and bend up the petals around the ball. Hold until set. (Be careful, glue can be hot!) Repeat for 1 pink flower and 1 lavender flower; set aside the other flowers.

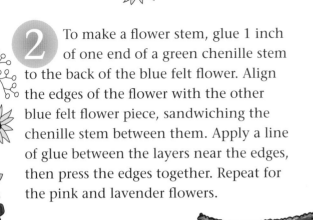

2 To make a flower stem, glue 1 inch of one end of a green chenille stem to the back of the blue felt flower. Align the edges of the flower with the other blue felt flower piece, sandwiching the chenille stem between them. Apply a line of glue between the layers near the edges, then press the edges together. Repeat for the pink and lavender flowers.

3 Add veins on the leaves with green dimensional paint; let dry. Glue 5 leaves to 3 flower stems; set aside the remaining leaf.

4 Add sprigs of gypsophila among the flowers. Make a bow out of the yellow ribbon. Wrap the remaining chenille stem around the middle of the bow, then wrap the chenille stem around all the flower stems. Twist the chenille stem ends together in the back, then trim and fold over the ends. Glue the remaining leaf to the back of the uppermost flower.

Patterns

Funky Foam Purse

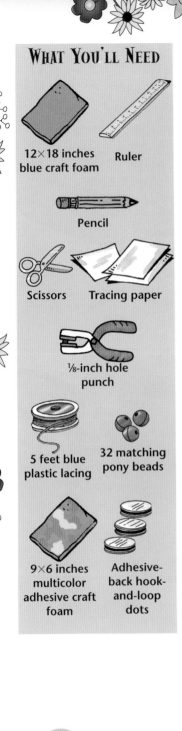

What You'll Need

12×18 inches blue craft foam

Ruler

Pencil

Scissors

Tracing paper

⅛-inch hole punch

5 feet blue plastic lacing

32 matching pony beads

9×6 inches multicolor adhesive craft foam

Adhesive-back hook-and-loop dots

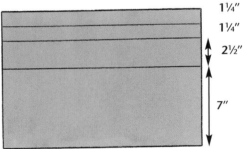

1¼"
1¼"
2½"
7"

1 Along the shorter edge of the blue foam, measure and mark 2 strips 1¼ inches wide (for the strap) and 1 strip 2½ inches wide. Cut out the strips. Using the pattern on page 9, trace and cut out 2 side panels from the 2½-inch-wide strip (copy the pattern markings). The remaining foam piece should measure about 7 inches wide. This will be for the pouch. Round the corners of the pouch piece on one side.

2 Starting ¼ inch from the squared edge of the pouch piece, measure and mark 26 points ½ inch apart and ¼ inch in from the side edge. Repeat on the other side. Punch holes at all points on all the pieces, including the side panels where indicated.

3 Cut a 36-inch length of plastic lacing. Line up the square edge of one side panel with one edge of the pouch piece. Thread the lacing through the first holes of each section, and leave a 10-inch tail on the side panel side. Continue lacing through the matching holes, using a basic sewing stitch, until all the holes are used. Be sure to keep the edges even and leave a 10-inch tail. Repeat on the other side.

4 Thread each tail through the top 2 holes on the side panel (the lace ends should end up on the outside of the side panel). Position one end of a strap piece over the holes at the top of a side panel. Use a pencil to mark points through the punched holes of the side panel to help you punch holes on the strap. Thread one lace end through the top hole on the strap, then thread the same lace diagonally to the bottom hole on the strap. Repeat with the other lace end (lace should have formed an *X*). Thread the lace ends through the opposite bottom strap holes. Tie the ends in a knot. Thread 3 pony beads on the remaining lacing, and tie a double knot on each end to hold the beads in place. Trim excess lacing. Repeat on the other side.

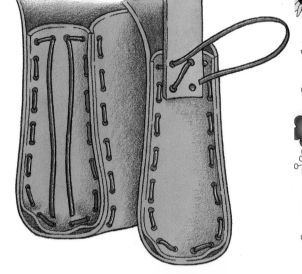

5 Overlap the straps to desired length to fit over your shoulder. Holding the strap pieces in place, punch 4 holes in a square about ½ inch apart and about ¼ inch from the edges of the straps. Cut a 12-inch length of lacing, then thread the lacing down through one bottom hole and up through the other bottom hole. Bring the ends together evenly, cross the lace ends to form an *X*, then thread them down through the top holes. Lace each end back up through the bottom holes, then tie a knot to hold in place. Thread 2 pony beads on each end of the lacing, and tie a double knot on each end to hold the beads in place. Trim excess lacing. Repeat on the other overlapped section of the strap.

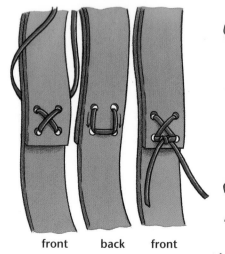

front   back   front

Patterns

6 Trace and cut out 3 flowers from the multicolor craft foam using the pattern on this page. Copy all markings, and punch holes at the points. Using 4 inches of lacing for each flower, thread the length of lacing through the holes, then tie a knot. Thread 2 pony beads on each end of the lacing, and tie a double knot at each end to hold the beads in place. Remove paper backing and stick the flowers to desired locations on the purse. Remove the paper backing from the loop dots and place them under the purse flap. Press the hook dots on the loop dots, then remove the backing from the hook dots and attach them to the front of the purse.

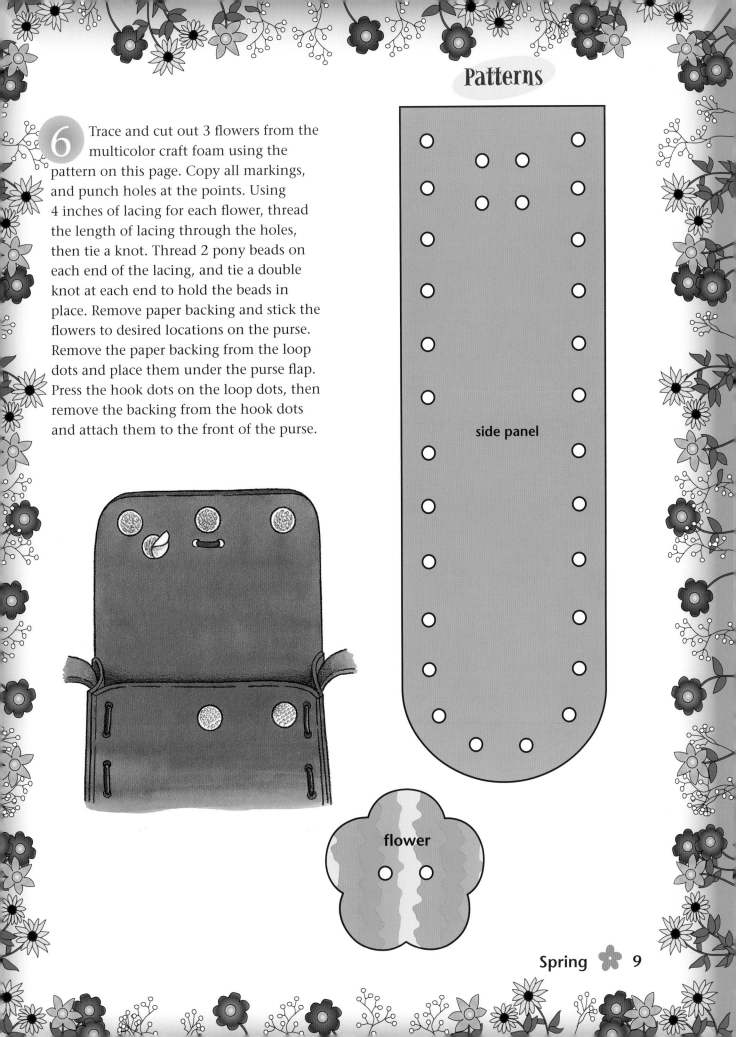

side panel

flower

Lucky Sprouts

What You'll Need

Compressed sponge

Pencil

Scissors

Plate or pie pan

Seeds

Quick-sprout seeds, such as cress or alfalfa

Spoon

Plastic wrap

Markers (optional)

1 Use the pattern on page 11 to trace and cut out a shamrock shape from the compressed sponge. Dampen the sponge so it expands, and squeeze out any extra water. Set the sponge on the plate or pie pan, and sprinkle the seeds on top of the sponge.

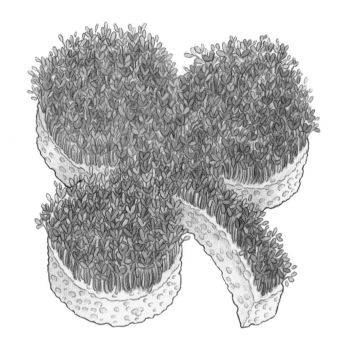

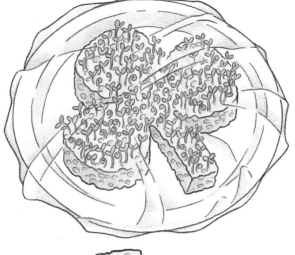

2 Your seeds should sprout in a few days (see instructions on the seed package) if you take good care of them! During the night, cover the sponge lightly with plastic wrap to help it stay moist. During the day, place your sponge in a sunny spot, making sure the sponge stays wet (water around the sponge; do not put water directly on the seeds).

3 For variety, draw and cut out different shapes from the compressed sponge. You can even try sprinkling seeds over just certain areas of the sponge. For example, you could cut out a shape that looks like a person's head and draw on a face with markers. Then sprinkle the seeds over the area where hair would grow. Pretend he's a leprechaun for even more luck!

Pattern

Did You Know?
The first St. Patrick's Day parade took place not in Ireland but in New York City on March 17, 1762.

May Day Colorful Lei

What You'll Need

Yarn

Scissors

Construction paper

Pencil

Hole punch

Pony beads or any large beads

Tape (optional)

1 Cut a length of yarn to hang loosely around your neck (make sure you cut it a little longer than you want it so you have room to tie the ends of the yarn together).

Use the patterns on page 13 to trace and cut about 3 dozen colorful flower shapes from construction paper. (If you want flowers that will stand up to a little more wear and tear, make them out of craft foam; use tissue paper for more delicate flowers.) Punch a hole in the center of each flower.

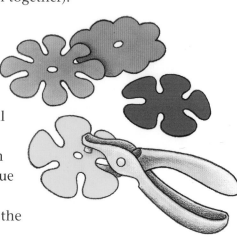

2 Tie a knot at one end of the piece of yarn. String 6 to 10 beads onto the yarn (this will be the part of the lei that touches the back of your neck). Then alternate flowers and beads however you want. If you have a hard time stringing the beads onto the yarn, wrap a small piece of tape around the end of the yarn to stiffen it.

3 Once you get the design you want and the yarn is almost full of flowers and beads, end just as you started, with 6 to 10 beads. Tie the end in a knot. Then tie the two ends of the yarn together, and wear your lei with pride!

Did You Know?

May Day is celebrated as a festival marking the reappearance of flowers during the spring. People in Hawaii celebrate May Day by giving flower leis to each other.

Patterns

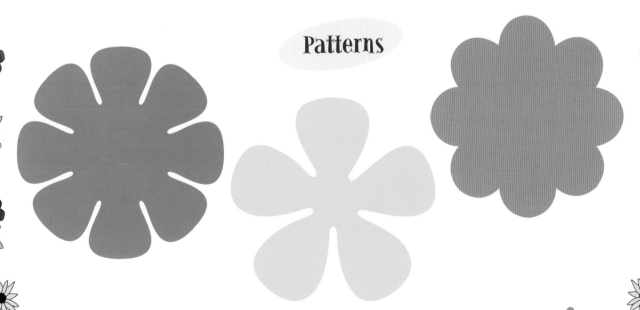

Maraca Mania

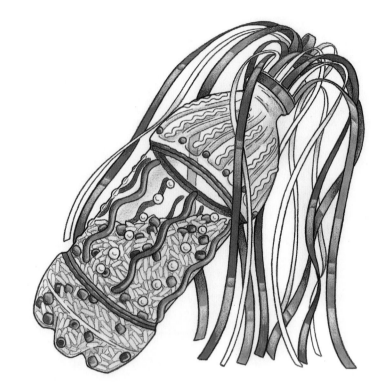

WHAT YOU'LL NEED

Clean, empty 16-ounce plastic bottle with cap

Funnel or paper

⅓ cup rice

Beads: ⅓ cup each red, green, white

Glitter or sequins: few teaspoons each red, green, white

Glue

Ribbon: red, green, white

Scissors

Fabric paint: red, green, white

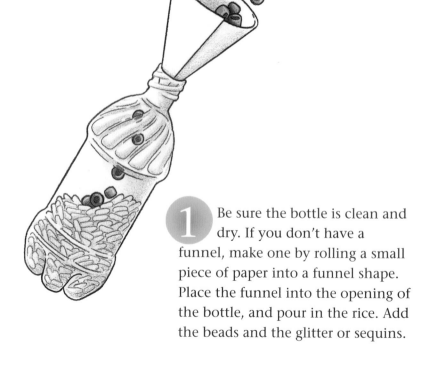

① Be sure the bottle is clean and dry. If you don't have a funnel, make one by rolling a small piece of paper into a funnel shape. Place the funnel into the opening of the bottle, and pour in the rice. Add the beads and the glitter or sequins.

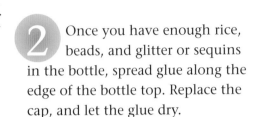

2 Once you have enough rice, beads, and glitter or sequins in the bottle, spread glue along the edge of the bottle top. Replace the cap, and let the glue dry.

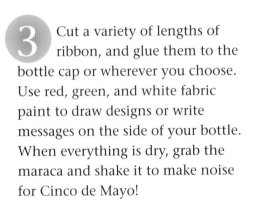

3 Cut a variety of lengths of ribbon, and glue them to the bottle cap or wherever you choose. Use red, green, and white fabric paint to draw designs or write messages on the side of your bottle. When everything is dry, grab the maraca and shake it to make noise for Cinco de Mayo!

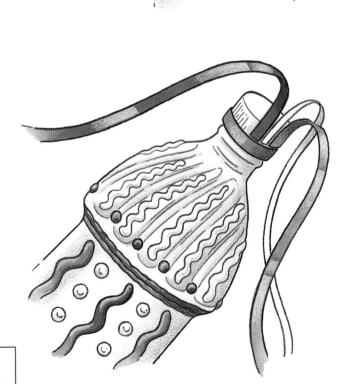

Did You Know?

Cinco de Mayo, which means "Fifth of May" in Spanish, is a holiday to celebrate the Mexican Army's victory over the French at the Battle of Puebla on May 5, 1862.

Cool Camp Frame

Adult help needed

1 Ask an adult to help you take apart the wood frame, and set aside the frame backing and glass. Use sandpaper to remove any rough edges on the wood frame. Wipe the frame with a soft cloth to remove dust, then paint the frame in the desired color with a paintbrush. Let dry 2 hours.

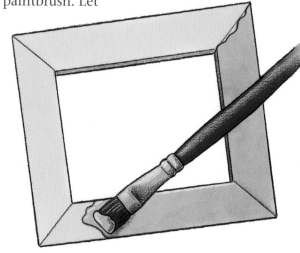

2 Arrange 13 craft picks on a flat surface for the camp sign, alternating the direction of the picks as shown. Lay 2 craft picks across the sign vertically, and cut off any excess wood. Glue the 2 picks to the sign; let dry 2 hours. Paint the sign the desired color. Let dry 1 hour, then use permanent markers to write your name, "Camp is Fun!," or anything else you want.

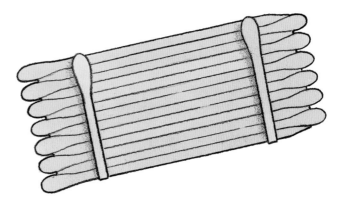

3 To make the head of the boy or girl, measure and cut 1½ inches from the smallest end of the craft spoon. Sand any rough edges. Refer to the illustration to cut craft picks for the hair, ears, and fingers. Paint the head, fingers (if you're making a boy), ears, and hair the desired colors. Let dry 1 hour. Glue the hair and ears onto the head. Use the markers to add a face.

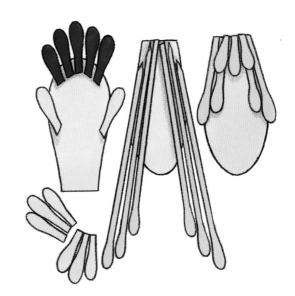

4 Glue the head (and fingers for a boy) to the sign, then glue the sign to the top of the frame. Let dry 2 hours. Paint all the wood with the waterbase varnish. Let dry 1 hour or as directed by the manufacturer. If you're making a girl, tie the ribbon in a bow and glue it to the top of the head. Have an adult help you put the frame back together. Be sure to insert a camp photo in the frame to show how much fun you had this summer!

Festive Fireworks T-shirt

Clean, white T-shirt

Cardboard

Scissors

2 spray bottles

Water

Measuring cup

Red and blue fabric paint, 1 ounce each

Paintbrush

1 Be sure to cover yourself and your work area—this is a very messy project! You may even want to work outside. Cut a piece of cardboard so it fits inside the T-shirt, and slide the cardboard inside the shirt. This will prevent the paint from soaking through from one side to the other. Lay the shirt flat on your work surface.

2 Add about ⅓ cup of water to each spray bottle. Empty most of the red fabric paint into 1 spray bottle. Empty most of the blue paint into the other spray bottle. You need to thin the paint just enough so it can be squirted out of the bottle, so you may need to add more water (add just a small amount of water at a time).

3 Now for the really fun part! Spray red and blue starburst designs onto the shirt until it looks the way you want it. Wait for one side of the shirt to dry (about 1 hour), then flip over the shirt and spray the other side. Let dry.

4 Use a paintbrush and the remaining fabric paint to highlight different areas of your design. Let dry. Wear your shirt on the Fourth of July—or any day—with pride! (To care for your shirt, wash it in cold water and hang it up or lay it flat to dry.)

On-the-Go Lap Desk

WHAT YOU'LL NEED

9×12-inch chalkboard

Pencil

Red acrylic paint

Small paintbrush

White paint pen

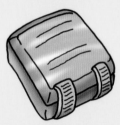

2-inch-deep plastic container, less than 9×12 inches

Low-temperature glue gun, glue sticks

1 Trace and cut out the pattern on page 21, then trace the star shape on the front of the chalkboard as many times as you want to create a nice design.

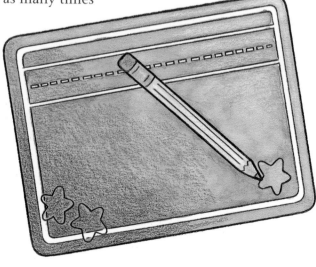

2 Paint the star shapes with the red paint. Let dry, then apply another coat of paint. Add small white detail lines around each star with the paint pen.

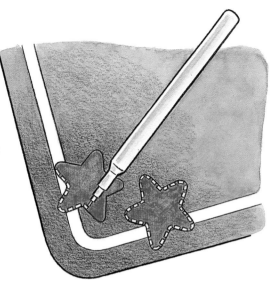

3 Center the chalkboard over the top of the container, then glue it in place. Let dry. Fill your lap desk with everything you need for a summer road trip!

Try This!

Instead of a plastic container, you could glue your decorated chalkboard on top of a pillow or a fabric pouch filled with small beans or foam pellets.

Pattern

Funtime Flip-Flops

Adult help needed

What You'll Need

Foam flip-flops

 2-yard length grosgrain or woven ribbon, 2 inches wide

Scissors

 Low-temperature glue gun, glue sticks

2 plastic or silk flowers (about 1 to 2 inches diameter) or 2 small plastic frogs

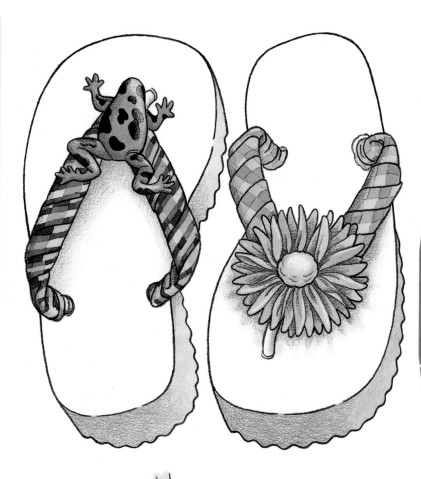

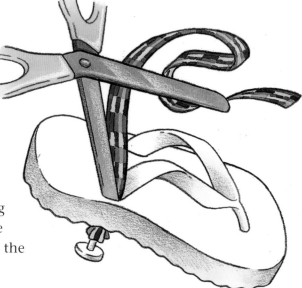

1 Cut the ribbon into 2 equal lengths. Loosen a side of a flip-flop thong by pushing it down through the bottom of the shoe. Ask an adult to help you use the tip of the scissors to poke the end of a length of ribbon through the hole on that side. Pull the ribbon so about 1 inch hangs underneath the flip-flop. Using the glue gun, fill the hole with glue, then pull up the thong so it fits back into the hole on the bottom. Be sure the end of the ribbon is still visible from the bottom of the shoe.

2 Working on the top of the flip-flop, wrap the ribbon around the thong so the plastic is completely covered. Overlap the edges each time you wrap the ribbon around to make sure it's secure. When you reach the other side of the thong, secure the end of the ribbon through the hole of the flip-flop as you did in step 1.

3 If you are making flower flip-flops, trim the stems from the plastic flowers. Using the glue gun, attach the flower or frog to the center of the thong. Repeat all steps for the other flip-flop.

Try This!

Don't stop with frogs or flowers. You can make all kinds of fun flip-flops using plastic bugs, cute erasers, or whatever else you dream up!

Totally Buggy Clips

WHAT YOU'LL NEED

Pencil

Craft foam scraps

Scissors

Craft glue

Hole punch

1-inch colored clothespins

Clear fishing line

2 thumbtacks

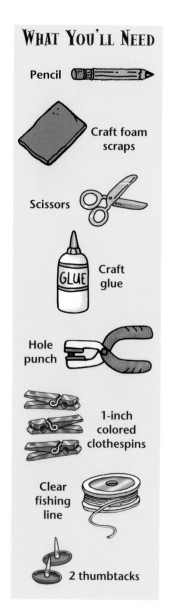

1 Use the patterns on page 26 to trace and cut out bug shapes of various colors from craft foam.

2 To make a ladybug, glue 2 ladybug wings on top of a ladybug body, keeping the wings slightly apart in the middle. Use the hole punch to make small circles out of craft foam; glue them to the top of the ladybug wings. For the butterfly and dragonfly, glue a body cutout to a wing cutout. Let dry.

3 Turn the bugs over, and glue a clothespin to the back of each bug. Let dry. String the fishing line along a wall, and secure it with a thumbtack on each end. Clip your buggy clothespins onto the line to hang your very best photos and artwork!

Try This!
Instead of mini clothespins, glue the buggy foam shapes onto adhesive-back magnet strips. Then use them to display your best artwork or top-notch tests on the refrigerator for all to see!

Patterns

Wingin' It

WHAT YOU'LL NEED

6-foot length clear
plastic lanyard

24mm split ring

Beads: 26 royal blue baby
pony, 2 black glitter pony,
14 purple glitter pony,
34 light blue baby pony,
22 lavender baby pony,
10 blue glitter pony

Nail clippers

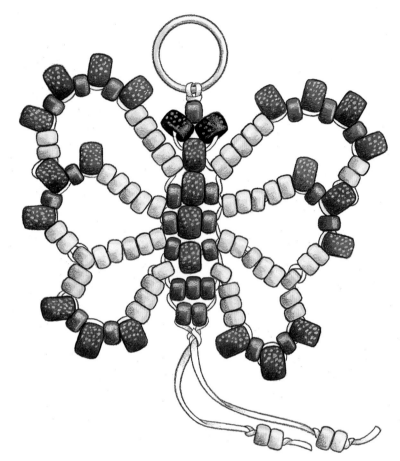

1 Fold the lanyard in half, and slip the looped end through the split ring. Pull the cut ends up through the loop and pull tight. String a royal blue baby pony bead onto the left strand and slide it all the way up. Weave the right strand through the bead from right to left. String 1 black glitter pony bead onto each strand for the eyes, then add a purple glitter pony bead to the left strand. Weave the right strand through the purple glitter bead from right to left. Be sure to keep the lanyard flat as you weave it from one row to the next.

2 To make the first "sidepath" of the right butterfly wing, string beads 1–15 on the right strand. Leave a little space between the beads, and weave back through, skipping the larger beads (beads 12, 10, 8, and 6). Pull tightly as you weave back, allowing the beads to curve as shown. Repeat to make the first sidepath of the left butterfly wing with the left strand. Add 1 royal blue baby pony, 1 purple glitter pony, and 1 royal blue baby pony to the left strand. Weave the right strand through the same 3 beads right to left.

3 String the second sidepath on each side of the butterfly. As you weave back toward the body, make sure to skip bead 15 from the first sidepath. Similarly, after stringing the third sidepath, skip bead 12 from the middle sidepath as you weave back toward the body.

4 Lace the last bead (16) of both lower wings to the body as a bead between rows. Use the bead diagram on the top of page 28 to finish the last 2 rows.

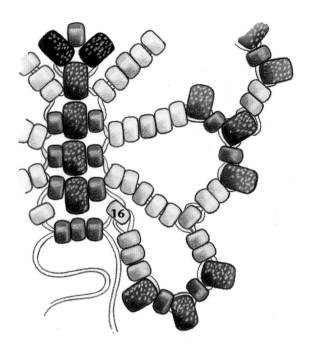

5 Tie the lanyard ends together in an overhand knot. To do this, twist both lanyard ends into a loop and then pull the free ends through the loop. Tie a double knot toward the end of each strand. Thread a lavender bead and a light blue bead on each end, then tie a double knot on each strand to hold the beads in place (see illustration on page 27). Trim excess lanyard with nail clippers, leaving ¼-inch ends.

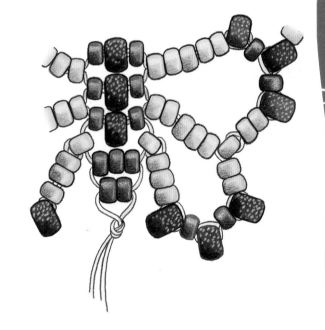

Try This!
Once you have the basic beading techniques down, use different color beads to create all kinds of butterflies. Try making a monarch with orange, black, and white beads.

What You'll Need

- Ruler
- Pencil
- Foam core
- Craft knife
- Craft glue
- Scrapbook paper
- Matching ribbon
- Scissors
- Velcro hook-and-loop fasteners

Adult help needed

Bulletin Board

1 Measure the width of the inside of your locker door, and subtract 1 inch to determine the width of the bulletin board. The height for the board is 11 inches. Lay the foam core flat, then ask an adult to help you mark and cut out 2 pieces of foam core with the craft knife according to your measurements. Glue the pieces together, one on top of the other.

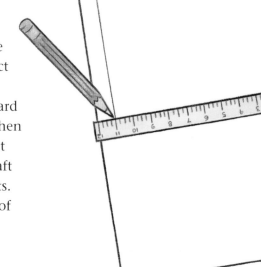

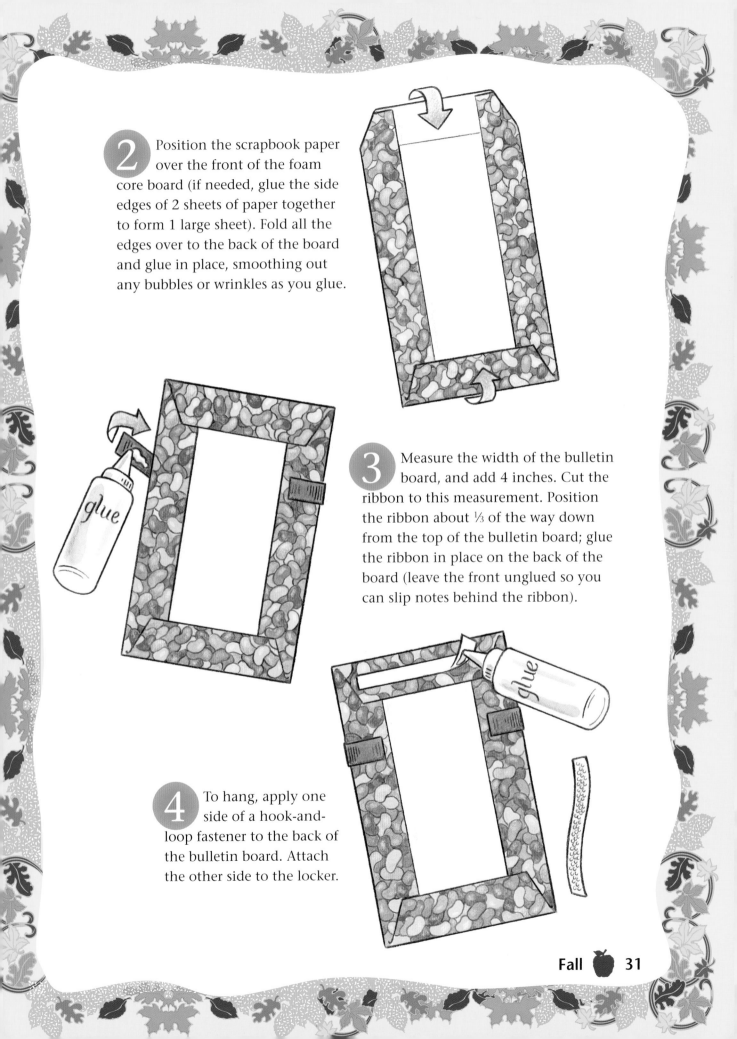

2 Position the scrapbook paper over the front of the foam core board (if needed, glue the side edges of 2 sheets of paper together to form 1 large sheet). Fold all the edges over to the back of the board and glue in place, smoothing out any bubbles or wrinkles as you glue.

3 Measure the width of the bulletin board, and add 4 inches. Cut the ribbon to this measurement. Position the ribbon about ⅓ of the way down from the top of the bulletin board; glue the ribbon in place on the back of the board (leave the front unglued so you can slip notes behind the ribbon).

4 To hang, apply one side of a hook-and-loop fastener to the back of the bulletin board. Attach the other side to the locker.

Notebook Cover

1 Position the scrapbook paper over the front of a notebook (if needed, glue the side edges of 2 sheets of paper together to form 1 large sheet). Cut a notch at the top and bottom of the paper where the notebook's spine falls. Then turn all the edges to the inside of the notebook and glue in place, smoothing out any bubbles and wrinkles as you glue.

2 Measure the width of the open notebook, then add 16 inches. Cut the ribbon to this measurement. Position the ribbon around the center front and back of the notebook, and glue in place. When dry, tie the ribbons together at the book's opening edge.

Try This!
You can make Back-to-School Beauties out of lots of things—mini notepads, pencil cases, you name it! Just follow the basic techniques listed for the bulletin board and notebook cover.

Halloween Mobile

What You'll Need

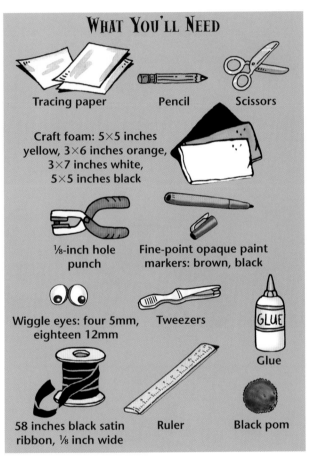

Tracing paper   Pencil   Scissors

Craft foam: 5×5 inches
yellow, 3×6 inches orange,
3×7 inches white,
5×5 inches black

⅛-inch hole
punch

Fine-point opaque paint
markers: brown, black

Wiggle eyes: four 5mm,
eighteen 12mm

Tweezers

Glue

58 inches black satin
ribbon, ⅛ inch wide

Ruler

Black pom

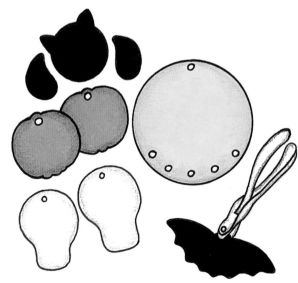

1 Using the patterns on page 35, trace and cut out the following shapes from the craft foam: 1 yellow moon, 2 orange pumpkins (one of each pattern), 2 white skulls, 1 black bat, 1 black cat head, and 2 black cat paws. Use the hole punch to make holes in the foam shapes as shown on the patterns.

2 Draw lines on both sides of the pumpkins with the brown marker; use the black marker to make faces on both sides. Let dry. Draw faces on both sides of the skulls with the black marker; let dry. Use tweezers to glue two 5mm eyes on both sides of the bat. Glue two 12mm eyes on both sides of the pumpkins and skulls.

3 Cut a 12-inch length of ribbon. Insert one end of the ribbon 1½ inches into the single hole at the top of the moon. Tie a double knot in the ribbon to securely attach it to the moon. Trim the short end of the ribbon close to the knot. Position and glue the cat head on the back upper side of the moon. Position and glue the cat paws on the front of the moon. Glue the black pom nose on the cat head so it slightly overlaps the edge of the moon, and glue two 12mm eyes to the cat head.

4 Cut the remaining ribbon into the following lengths, and use double knots to tie one end of each length to a foam shape and the other end to a hole at the bottom of the moon: 6-inch length for 1 pumpkin, 9-inch length for 1 skull, 13-inch length for the bat; 11-inch length for 1 pumpkin, 7-inch length for 1 skull. Trim the ends of each length of ribbon close to the knots.

34 🍎 **Fall**

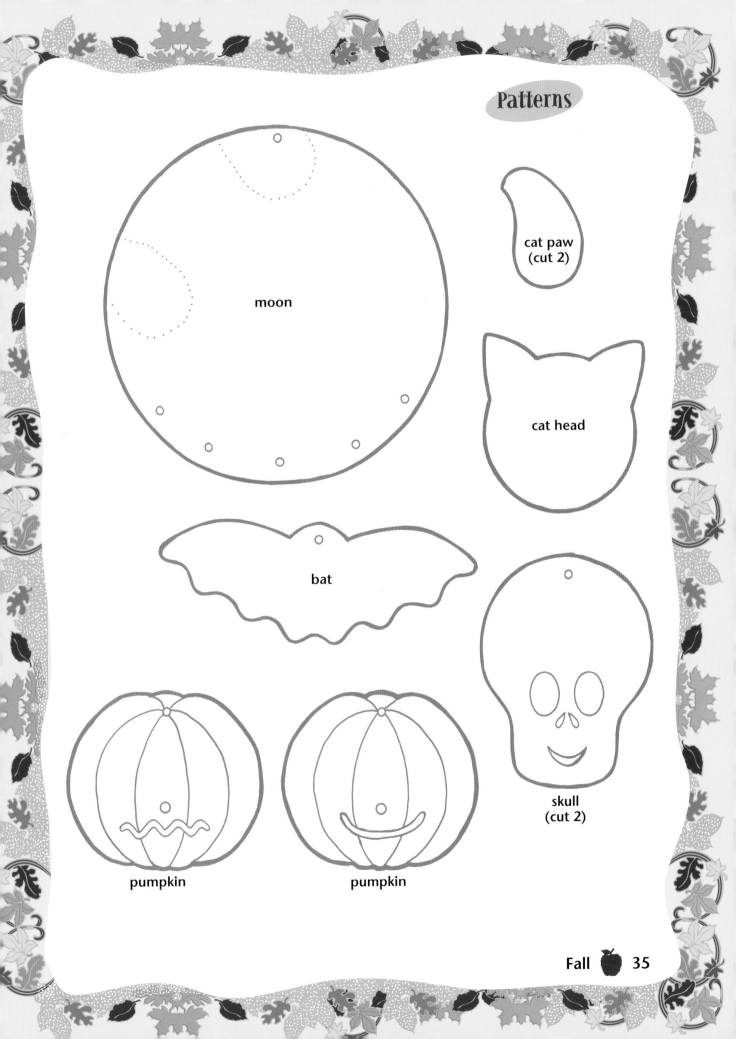

Patterns

moon

cat paw
(cut 2)

cat head

bat

skull
(cut 2)

pumpkin

pumpkin

Veggie Magnets

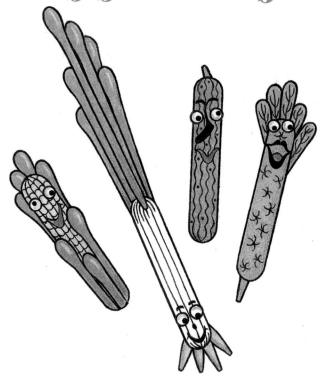

What You'll Need

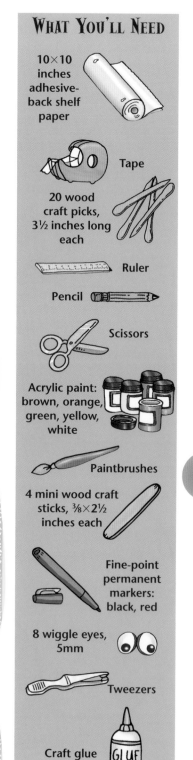

10×10 inches adhesive-back shelf paper

Tape

20 wood craft picks, 3½ inches long each

Ruler

Pencil

Scissors

Acrylic paint: brown, orange, green, yellow, white

Paintbrushes

4 mini wood craft sticks, ⅜×2½ inches each

Fine-point permanent markers: black, red

8 wiggle eyes, 5mm

Tweezers

Craft glue

½×2½-inch strip adhesive-back magnet

1 Remove the backing from the shelf paper and place it on a flat surface with the adhesive side up. Use tape to hold down the corners. Measure and mark ½ inch from the pointed ends of 5 craft picks. Cut each pick at the marking. Place the pointed pieces on the shelf paper to hold while painting. Paint 4 pointed pieces brown for the onion roots and 1 piece orange for the tip of the carrot. Lay all the remaining craft picks and sticks on the shelf paper, leaving a little space between each piece. Paint the remaining craft picks green. Refer to the illustration to paint the mini craft sticks for each vegetable. Let dry 1 hour, then turn over and paint the back sides. Let dry 1 hour.

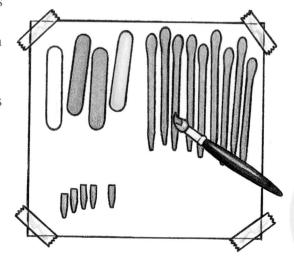

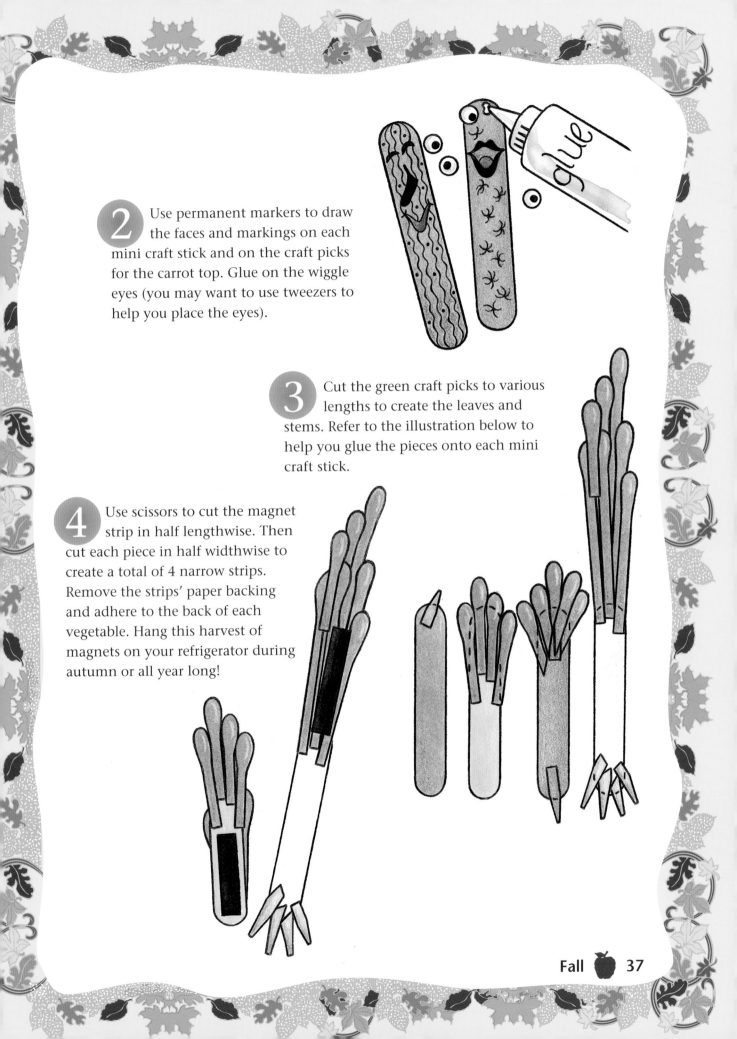

2 Use permanent markers to draw the faces and markings on each mini craft stick and on the craft picks for the carrot top. Glue on the wiggle eyes (you may want to use tweezers to help you place the eyes).

3 Cut the green craft picks to various lengths to create the leaves and stems. Refer to the illustration below to help you glue the pieces onto each mini craft stick.

4 Use scissors to cut the magnet strip in half lengthwise. Then cut each piece in half widthwise to create a total of 4 narrow strips. Remove the strips' paper backing and adhere to the back of each vegetable. Hang this harvest of magnets on your refrigerator during autumn or all year long!

Turkey Table Favor

WHAT YOU'LL NEED

1⅛-inch wood doll pin base

Wood balls: 1¾-inch diameter, 1¼-inch diameter

Wood teardrop cutouts: 11 large, 2 small

Acrylic paint: brown, yellow, red, orange

Paintbrushes

Low-temperature glue gun, glue sticks

Cardboard box

Acrylic spray sealer

Tracing paper

Pencil

Scissors

Felt: 1×2 inches orange, 1×2 inches red

2 wiggle eyes, 8mm each

Tweezers

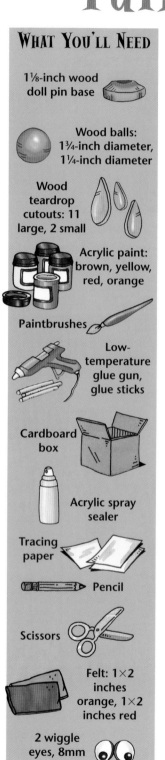

1 Paint the wood pieces in the following colors: doll pin base and both balls—brown; 4 large teardrops—yellow; 4 large teardrops—red; 3 large teardrops and 2 small teardrops—orange. Let dry, then apply a second coat of paint. Let dry completely.

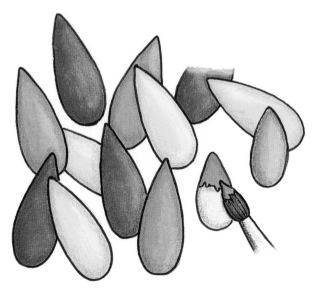

2 To make the turkey's body, glue the 1¾-inch ball to the doll pin base. For the head, glue the 1¼-inch ball to the front top of the body.

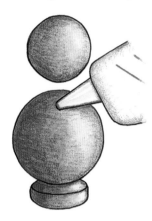

3 Arrange the large teardrop pieces as shown in the illustration for the turkey's feathers. Overlap the edges of the large teardrops, and glue them together so they form a half circle of feathers. Glue the half circle of feathers to the body at the center and at each end of the half circle. To make the wings, glue a small teardrop to each side of the body. Put the turkey in a cardboard box in a well-ventilated area, and have an adult help you lightly spray it with acrylic sealer. Let dry.

4 To make the beak, use the pattern below to trace and cut out 2 triangles from orange felt. Align the tops of each triangle, and glue them to the center front of the head. Use the pattern below to trace and cut out the wattle from red felt. Glue the top of the wattle to the head just below the beak. Glue the wiggle eyes to the turkey's head above the beak (use the tweezers to help you place them).

Patterns

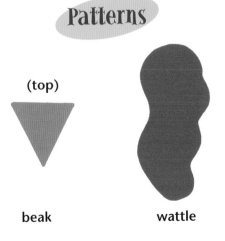

(top)

beak   wattle

Harvest Bookmark

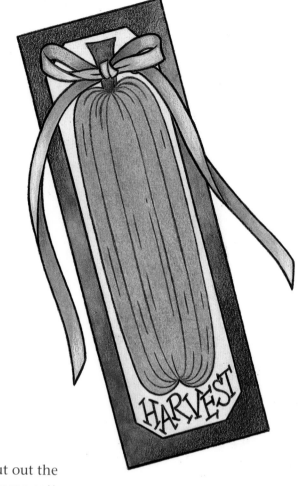

What You'll Need

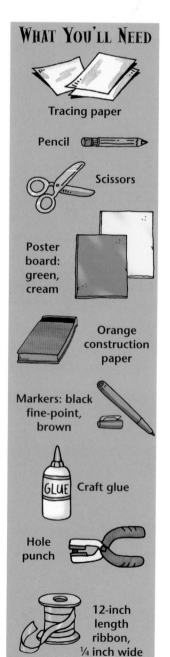

Tracing paper

Pencil

Scissors

Poster board: green, cream

Orange construction paper

Markers: black fine-point, brown

Craft glue

Hole punch

12-inch length ribbon, ¼ inch wide

1 Trace and cut out the bookmark frame pattern on page 41 from the green poster board. Repeat for the bookmark insert pattern from cream poster board and the pumpkin from orange construction paper. Add the detail lines on the pumpkin with black marker. Color the stem with brown marker.

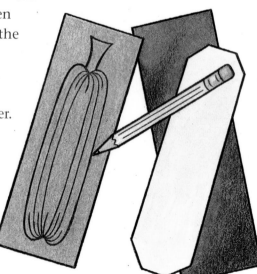

2 Glue the pieces together, stacking them on top of one another. Let dry 20 minutes. Write *HARVEST* below the pumpkin with black marker.

3 Punch holes on both sides of the stem, insert the ribbon through the holes, and tie a bow at the base of the stem.

Patterns

frame

insert

Bat-Wing Bracelet

1 Use the pattern on page 43 to trace and cut out 2 or 3 bats from black construction paper. Decorate the bats with puffy paints and glitter.

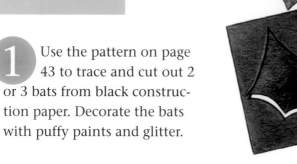

2 When the bats are completely dry, stack the bats on top of each other. Staple the bats together in the center.

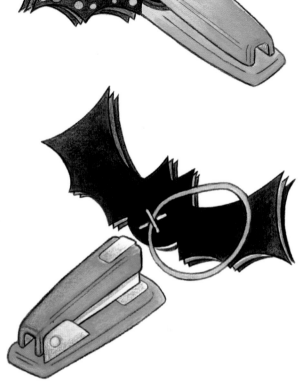

3 Place a rubber band over the back of the staple, and staple the rubber band to the bats. Fan out the bat wings, and wear around your wrist as a spooky accessory!

Pattern

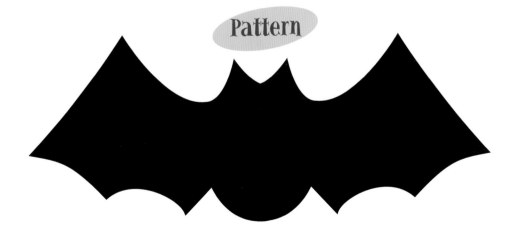

Christmas Window Decorations

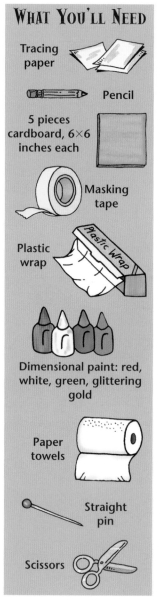

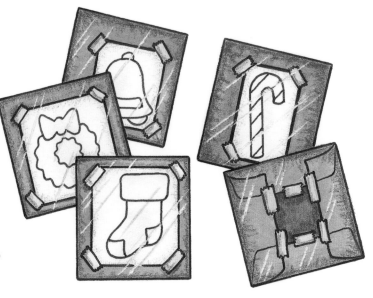

1 Trace the patterns on page 46 onto individual pieces of paper, then tape each piece of paper to a piece of cardboard. Tightly cover each pattern with plastic wrap, and tape the edges of the plastic wrap to the back of the cardboard.

2 Carefully paint the plastic wrap using the patterns as a guide (refer to the illustrations for color direction). Work with 1 color at a time, and let each color set for 10 minutes before you paint with the next color. Follow these tips for using dimensional paint: Outline the part of the pattern you're going to paint; lightly touch the tip of the bottle to the plastic wrap, carefully squeeze the bottle, and pull (don't push) the tip along the outline (the paint should be about ⅛ inch thick). Then paint inside the outlined area, working from left to right (or right to left if you're left-handed) and top to bottom. If you make a mistake, wipe off the paint with a paper towel. If the tip of the bottle clogs, use a straight pin to open the hole and then squeeze a bit of paint on paper scrap to regain a smooth flow.

3 Let the paint dry for 24 hours. Peel the decorations off the plastic wrap. Trim paint that has spread beyond the outline of the decorations. Place the decorations on your windows for happy holiday cheer!

Patterns

Sensational Spiral Ornament

What You'll Need

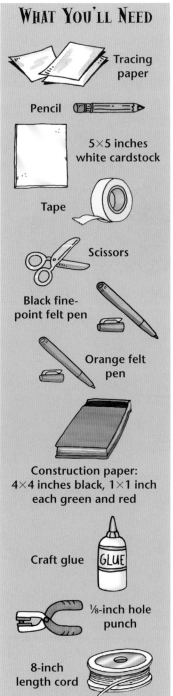

Tracing paper

Pencil

5×5 inches white cardstock

Tape

Scissors

Black fine-point felt pen

Orange felt pen

Construction paper: 4×4 inches black, 1×1 inch each green and red

Craft glue

⅛-inch hole punch

8-inch length cord

1 Trace or photocopy the patterns on page 48. Tape the spiral pattern to the cardstock, and cut along the lines of the pattern. Remove the pattern.

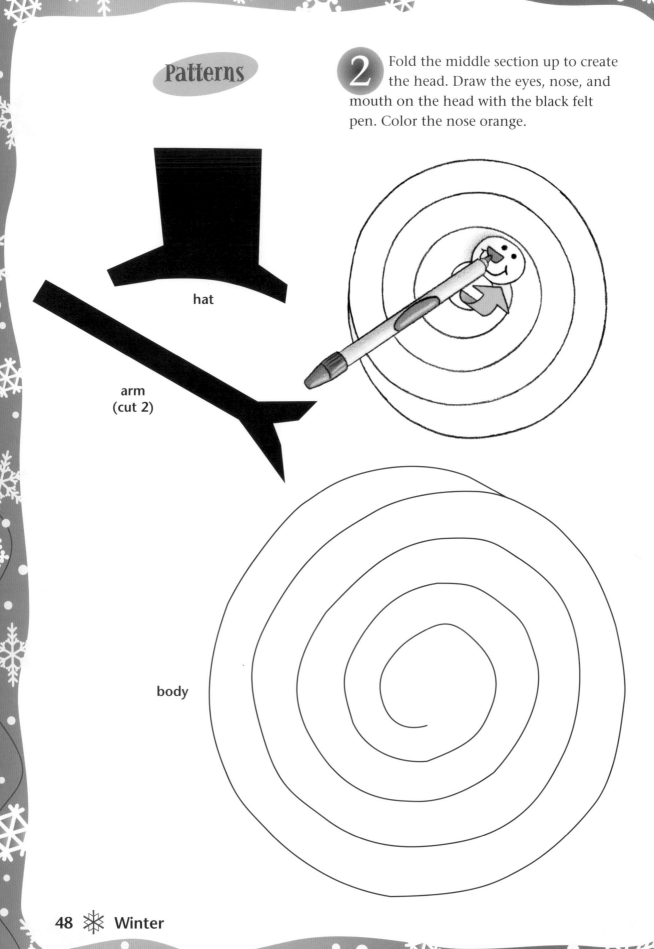

Patterns

2 Fold the middle section up to create the head. Draw the eyes, nose, and mouth on the head with the black felt pen. Color the nose orange.

hat

arm
(cut 2)

body

3 Cut out the patterns for the arm and the hat. Trace the arm pattern twice on black paper, and cut them out. Fold the remaining piece of black paper in half, and place the top edge of the hat pattern along the fold. Trace around the pattern, and cut it out (don't cut the fold). Apply glue to the inside of the hat, and slip it over the snowman's head. Press the hat pieces together, sandwiching the top of the head between them. Glue an arm to each side of the first spiral below the head.

4 From the green paper, cut out 2 holly leaves. Use the hole punch to make a red berry from the red paper. Glue the holly leaves and the berry to the hat.

5 Punch a hole in the top of the hat. Fold the cord in half, and tie the ends of the cord together. Push the cord loop through the hole, and thread the tied ends of the cord through the loop of the cord. Hang your spiral friend on a Christmas tree or wherever you like!

Adult help needed

WHAT YOU'LL NEED

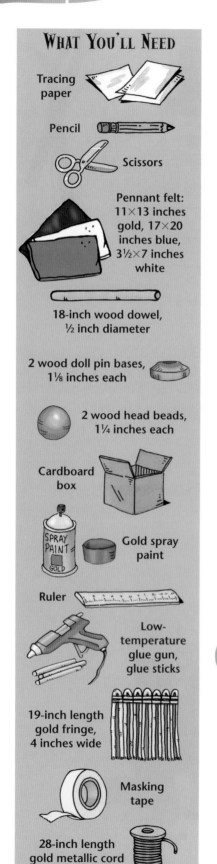

Tracing paper

Pencil

Scissors

Pennant felt: 11×13 inches gold, 17×20 inches blue, 3½×7 inches white

18-inch wood dowel, ½ inch diameter

2 wood doll pin bases, 1⅛ inches each

2 wood head beads, 1¼ inches each

Cardboard box

Gold spray paint

Ruler

Low-temperature glue gun, glue sticks

19-inch length gold fringe, 4 inches wide

Masking tape

28-inch length gold metallic cord

① Using the pattern on page 51, trace and cut out the menorah from the gold felt. Working with an adult in a well-ventilated area, place the menorah, the dowel, the 2 doll pin bases, and the 2 head beads in the cardboard box. Spray all with 2 coats of gold spray paint. Let dry between coats.

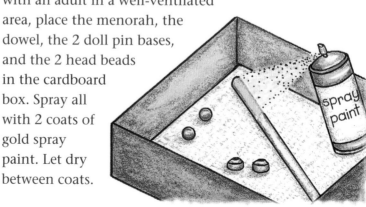

50 ❄ Winter

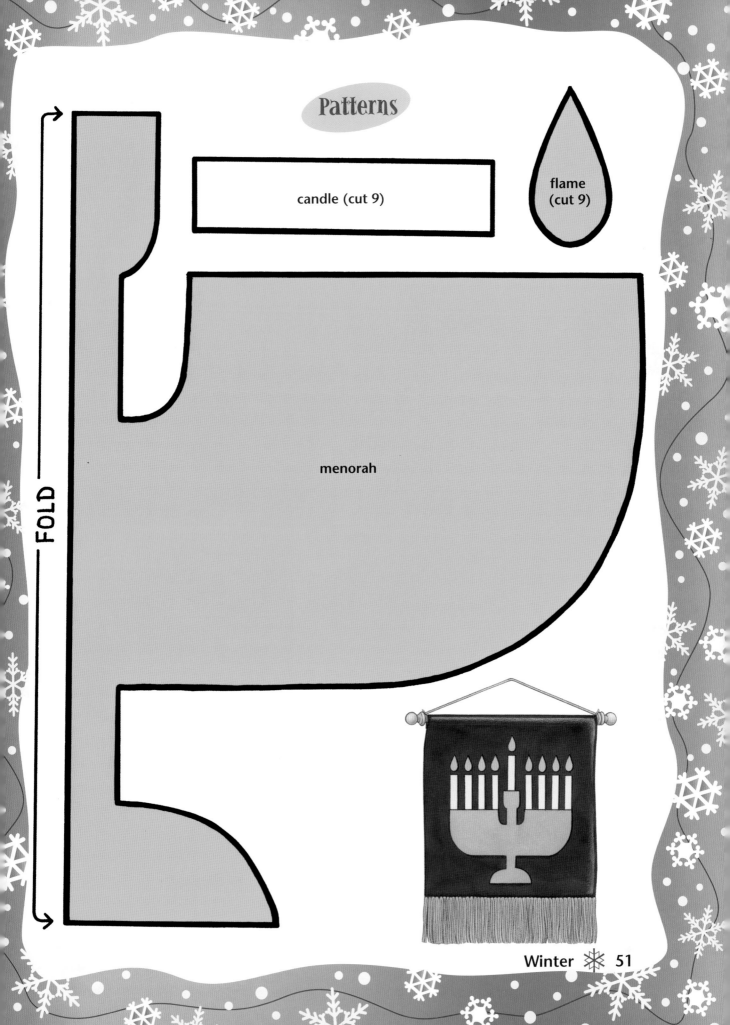

Patterns

candle (cut 9)

flame
(cut 9)

FOLD

menorah

2 Fold over 2 inches of a 17-inch edge of blue felt, and crease it. Unfold, then apply a line of glue 3¾ inches down from the top edge. Refold the felt, and hold it in place until the glue dries. Be sure to leave enough room between the crease and the glue line to insert the dowel. This fold is the top.

4 Glue the fringe to the bottom of the banner so 1 inch of fringe sticks out from each side. Fold and glue the excess fringe to the back of the banner. Position the menorah and candles as shown in the illustration, then glue them to the banner. For each day of Hanukkah, roll a piece of masking tape into a loop with the sticky side out, put it on the back of a flame, and add the flame to the banner.

3 Using the patterns on page 51, trace and cut out 9 candles from the white pennant felt and 9 flames from the gold felt.

5 Slide the dowel through the hem at the top of the banner. Glue a head bead to a doll pin base, then glue them to one end of the dowel. Repeat on the other end of the dowel. To make a hanger, tie the ends of the cord to the ends of the dowel.

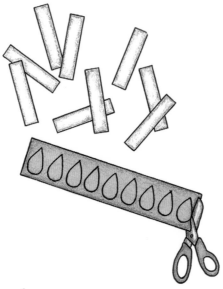

My Kwanzaa Family

Use the patterns on page 54 to cut out the father's body...

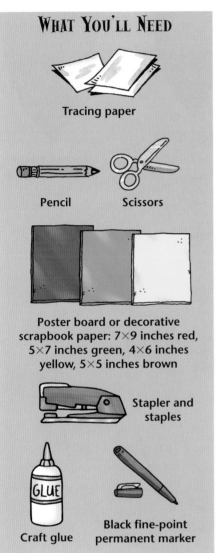

What You'll Need

Tracing paper

Pencil **Scissors**

Poster board or decorative scrapbook paper: 7×9 inches red, 5×7 inches green, 4×6 inches yellow, 5×5 inches brown

Stapler and staples

Craft glue **Black fine-point permanent marker**

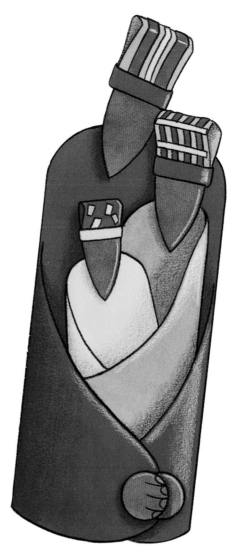

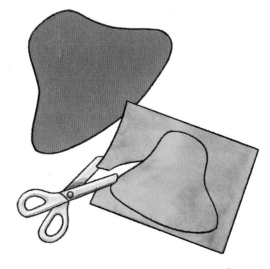

1 Use the patterns on page 54 to cut out the father's body from red poster board or scrapbook paper. Repeat for the mother's body pattern using green paper and the child's body pattern using yellow paper. Trace and cut out 2 head patterns for the mother and father, 1 child's head, and 2 father's hands from brown paper. Trace and cut out 2 hat patterns for the mother and father using green paper and 1 child's hat pattern from red paper. Set aside.

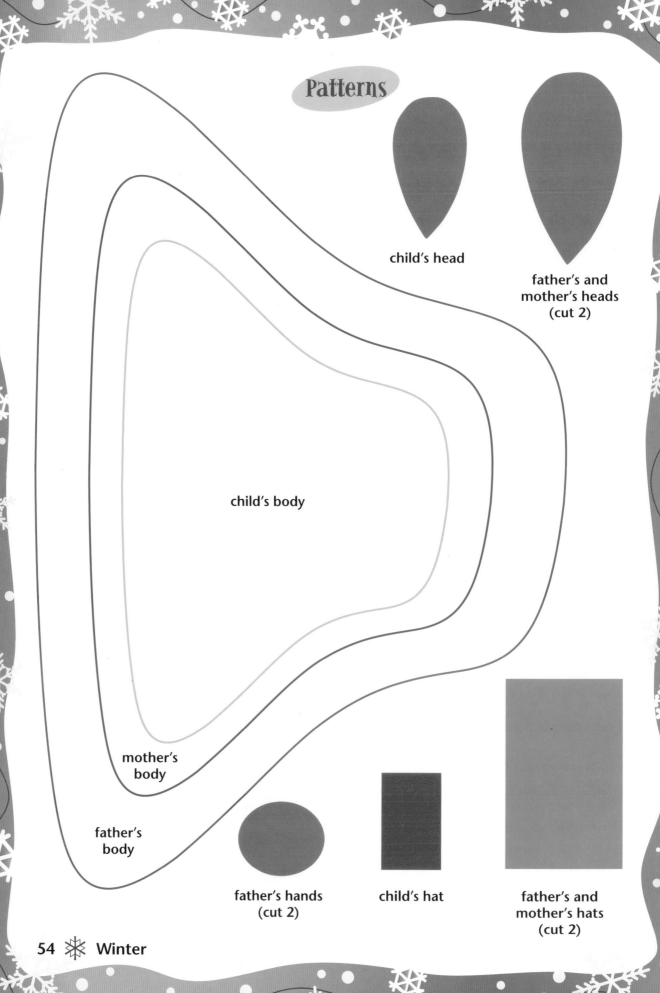

Patterns

child's head

father's and
mother's heads
(cut 2)

child's body

mother's
body

father's
body

father's hands
(cut 2)

child's hat

father's and
mother's hats
(cut 2)

2 Bring the "arm" parts of the father's "body" together, overlapping the arms in front and stapling them together. Repeat with mother and child cutouts. Glue heads onto the bodies of the mother, father, and child.

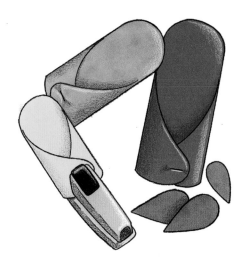

4 Insert the bodies one inside the other, turning them so the child is cradled at the center of the family. Draw the fingers on the father's hands with the black marker, then glue them to the front.

3 Decorate the hats with leftover paper or poster board scraps. Let dry. Fold the father's hat in half, bringing the short ends together, and staple or glue the hat to the father's head. Glue a strip of paper around the bottom of the hat to cover the staple. Repeat for the mother's and child's hats.

Did You Know?

Kwanzaa means "the first" or "the first fruits of the harvest" in Kiswahili. (Kiswahili is an East African language.) Dr. Maulana Karenga began the holiday in 1966 to celebrate the rich cultural roots of African-American people.

Heartbreaker

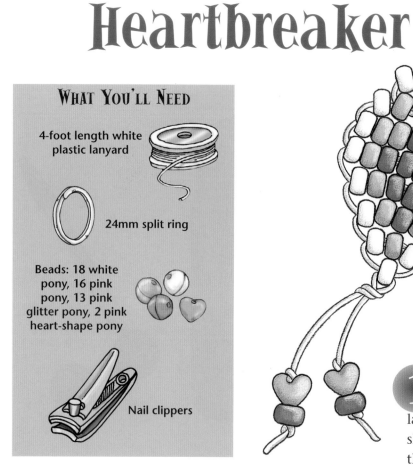

WHAT YOU'LL NEED

4-foot length white plastic lanyard

24mm split ring

Beads: 18 white pony, 16 pink pony, 13 pink glitter pony, 2 pink heart-shape pony

Nail clippers

1 Make a lark's head knot by folding the lanyard in half and slipping the looped end through the split ring. Pull the cut ends up through the loop; pull tight. Tie an overhand knot about ½ to 1 inch from the lark's head knot.

2 String a white bead onto the left strand, and slide it all the way up to the knot. Weave the right strand through the bead from right to left. To make the heart's upper arches, weave a "sidepath" by stringing beads 1–4 on the right strand. Leave a little space between the beads, and weave back through beads 1 and 2. Pull tightly as you weave back, allowing the beads to curve as shown. Repeat to make a sidepath with the left strand. Add a white bead on the end of each sidepath before you move on to the next row.

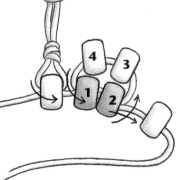

3 String beads onto the left strand in the following order: 1 white, 2 pink, 1 pink glitter, 1 pink, 1 pink glitter, 2 pink, and 1 white. Weave the right strand through the same beads from right to left. Repeat this basic bead-weaving technique for the remaining rows, using the bead diagram for reference.

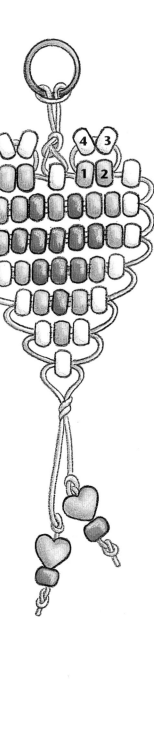

4 Finish by tying both cord ends together in an overhand knot. To do this, twist both lanyard ends into a loop and then pull the free ends through the loop. Tie a second overhand knot on each cord about 1½ to 2 inches from the first knot. String a heart pony bead and a glitter bead on each cord, and finish each with another overhand knot. Trim the excess cord with the nail clippers, leaving ½-inch tails.

Index

Letters preceding the page number correspond to one of the 4 individual books in this binder. R = *Rainy Day Crafts;* H = *Holiday Crafts;* A = *After School Crafts;* Y = *Year-Round Crafts for Kids.*